VHS COLLECTING
The Modern Relevance of Home Video

Written by Cory J. Gorski
Edited by Gregory Shanahan

Copyright © Cory J Gorski, 2020

All rights reserved. Without limiting the rights under copyright reserved above, no part of this publication may be reproduced, stored in or introduced into a retrieval system, or transmitted in any form or by any means (electronic, mechanical, photocopying, recording or otherwise), without the prior written permission of the copyright owner.

Print ISBN 9798632078504

CHAPTERS

Introduction
1. **Dawn of The Video Store**
2. **Fall of An Empire**
3. **A Perfect Collectible**
4. **Adjust Your Tracking**
5. **The Distributors**
6. **America's Most Wanted**
7. **The Good, The Bad & The Unwatchable**
8. **Rise of The Rip-offs**
9. **Think Outside the Box**
10. **Oh, The Horror!**
11. **The Video Dead**
12. **Vanishing Point**
13. **Attack of The Tapeheads**
14. **Be Kind — Rewind**

Introduction

"Why would anyone collect old VHS tapes?"
- Most people

VHS. Video Home System cassette. Yes, it's a dead format. Sure, tapes are inferior to DVD, Blu-ray, and digital. They take up a lot of physical space, but don't have much storage themselves. Sometimes...they even smell weird. All of this is true, yet you can still find collectors in thrift stores rummaging through old stacks of tapes. Why? Well, once you understand the retrospective history of home video, the nostalgia of a forgotten format and the thrill of the hunt combined with a rich appreciation for good *and* bad cinema, there will be no confusion. In fact, let's make a bet: after reading this book, you dig out the dusty old box of VHS tapes you have stashed away in your attic, if only to find out whether you own anything of value.

If you're already a casual VHS collector (which will be half of the people picking up this book), don't fret! There's plenty here relevant to your interests and I promise it won't be redundant. Even if you already know the general history, stay for the deep dive on why we collect certain tapes altogether. You'll find mention of a few of your favorite films/distributors/video stores and possibly gain a richer understanding of the subculture. With a little luck, you'll spiral further down the rabbit hole and become inspired enough to turn that spare room into a replica video store — complete with disgruntled spouse and maxed-out credit card.

Finally, if you're one of the old guard tapeheads who think someone writing a book about your secret hobby is exposing it to the world: remember that the internet exists. Tape collecting documentaries exist. VHS social media pages exist. In fact, those are far more widespread than an obscure book. So, relax. A stagnant culture is a dying one. Instead of locking yourself away in your parents' basement, dusting your VCR while drooling into darkness, let's instead remind society of the fantastic video format it was once completely enamored with. At its core, this is a love story — romanticizing the days of home video while celebrating the secret world of tape hoarders like you.

1. Dawn of The Video Store

Stop me if this sounds familiar: it's a Saturday night in the 1980s or early 1990s. It's about 10 pm and you're walking down the street with friends to grab food. Someone asks, "So, what do you want to do tonight?" The arcade and mall are closed. You're too young to go to bars or nightclubs, and you don't hang out at coffee shops. There are no parties this weekend, either. Internet gaming and escape rooms have yet to be invented. Perhaps you're even younger and just driving around town with your parents. It's dark out, and you're all bored, yet wide awake. The night is young, yet somehow void of entertainment. Suddenly, a light appears in the distance! It pierces the darkness, flashing a neon glow in the shape of a single word: "*OPEN*!".

The local video store. A narrow brick-and-mortar shop a few streets ahead. Its walls are lined with thousands of colorful rectangular boxes, each containing a film on magnetic tape that anyone with a membership card and a few dollars in their pocket can rent.

"Let's rent a flick!", suggests your friend or family member, pointing into the night. You make your way across a mostly empty parking lot, only to find a lively store, bright and vibrant. CRT television sets are playing trailers of upcoming movies. Dozens of racks line the walls, filled with hundreds of movies in cardboard slipcases, film posters peppered throughout the room. Fluorescent lights hover above, and a store clerk is chatting with a customer about a new action film. You nod to the employee as you walk by, bee-lining toward your favorite genre. As you peruse film boxes row by row, you hear someone call your name — an acquaintance you haven't seen in weeks! You make small talk, regroup with your friends/family, and start talking movies. It seems that the night has only just begun!

If you're of a certain vintage, the above scenario is probably something you've lived through. Youth of today might imagine the idea of physically renting a movie as tedious and laborious. However, you know better. The video store wasn't a chore, nor a hassle; it was a community. A *hub*. A meeting point around which to gather and celebrate film. It was an experience and discovery of new entertainment. Friends and family would congregate for an excursion into the fantastic world of cinema.

Sound like an exaggeration? Ask anyone who grew up with a video store in their neighborhood what the vibe was like. There wasn't a "get-in-get-out fast" mentality that many people have when shopping today. It was easy-going, relaxing and fun. It lacked the quiet and doldrum hush of a library. Quite the opposite. Unlike a bookstore, it could be exciting! Hundreds of new and old films presented for your enjoyment...and you could hold each one in the palm of your hand.

If one can attach meaning to physical music (i.e. vinyl records, cassettes, CDs), one could also attach meaning and value to physical video. Grab a tape, walk over to a friend and ask for their opinion. Its cover art would usher you into a unique little world. The synopsis on the back would cry out, begging you to explore the story hidden within. Sometimes, it lied. It was a gamble, since this was long before the days of easy access to film reviews. So, you talked to clerks, family and friends, doing your best to form an opinion on what to rent for the evening. That aspect was crucial — whatever you rented, chances are you were forced to watch it to completion. Even if it was terrible, you were stuck with it. If you only rented two films for the weekend, you watched both in their entirety. If it was truly awful...well, hopefully you had some alcohol handy.

Or, at least, someone with a sense of humor. Due to those limitations, it's very important to understand that *entertainment was consumed far differently than it is today.*

Appreciation for film, both the good and bad, simply had more depth. You didn't have the option of instantly skipping to another 499 films on Netflix. No, you had two options. You had the action flick and the screwball comedy your buddy picked out. That's it. Everybody watched bad films at some point, often against their will. You experienced shlocky shot-on-video trash. It was inevitable. However, once in a while you found that hidden gem on the bottom shelf. It was covered in dust, yet somehow it spoke to you. Perhaps you recognized the director or an actor who had recently made it big. Maybe you were instantly enamored by the bizarre and outlandish artwork. Whatever the reason, you slapped down your $2.99, proudly displayed your membership card and sat around howling all Saturday night with your new favorite flick. Score! It was a feeling of accomplishment because nobody instructed you to rent it. You made the discovery and could claim bragging rights after you brought it to the cottage to watch with your friends. People would now refer to certain types of movies as "*your*" films. It was a badge of honor. Others wore a badge of shame. "Oh no, another one of

Andrew's stinkers!", you might have heard when a group of friends discovered their companion was once again swindled by flashy box art and an all-too-promising synopsis. Andrew would become known as an untrustworthy film-flunky — a chump with poor taste in movies.

Finding any specific film was often a hunt. This may sound taxing and tedious, however, the phrase "thrill of the hunt" exists for a reason. Phoning all the local video stores in your neighborhood via landline telephone was something many hardcore film fans remember fondly. A basic question like, "Do you have a movie called *A Clockwork Orange* in stock?" could start up a conversation with a clerk that might last a while. At times, it could even instigate laughter. Something like, "Hello, I'm looking for a film called *Night of The Creeps*!" could invoke both gasps and giggles from a store employee. The thing is, when you finally tracked down that rare and obscure tape after *days* of calling around, you had a genuine feeling of accomplishment.

Choosing a film became part of the entertainment itself. If you were a child of the 1980s, you spent many nights simply perusing the video store even if you rented nothing. Many businesses offered free popcorn and played film trailers with behind-the-scenes featurettes. Life-size cardboard standees of the biggest action movie stars decorated the isles. Unique advertisements adorned the windows. Many had specialized areas, such as horror movie sections complete with scary mannequins and props. Relationships with clerks would form, if for no better reason than to simply get insider tips as to what was good, bad or downright terrible. Employees were often film buffs themselves and were given their own "Employee Picks" section featuring on-going personal film recommendations. The whole experience of choosing a film became an art form — developing a nuanced understanding of various genres and directors.

      If you were older at that time, chances are you had even more of an appreciation for home video. You could remember the days of being limited to only watching a film in theatres. Then, almost overnight, not only could you rent a film, but you could *own* it forever. This was a revolution for many and changed the way films were produced altogether. Many films were suddenly shot on video exclusively for the home market. People who had no experience directing movies suddenly found themselves at the helm of small film crews. Startup production houses formed in garages and distribution companies assembled in small warehouses. A boom cycle had begun. For the first time in history, any individual with enough drive, passion, and cash could take the summer off work and create a cheesy low-budget flick destined for VHS tape. With a little sweat, they could distribute it through mom-and-pop video stores across the country.

At the beginning of this era, stores only *sold* video, and for quite a high price. The idea was simple: you could buy your favorite movie for $79.99 - $99.99 USD and watch it in the comfort of your own home. What a novel idea! However, as you might imagine, such a price tag acted as a deterrent for much of the public. Tapes sold, but they weren't exactly flying off the shelf. Over time, it made more sense for businesses to charge a smaller fee and simply *rent* out the tape for a few days. Instead of dropping a hundred dollars to watch *The Shining*, you could rent it for three or four dollars and simply bring it back three days later! This model took over the industry and what was originally designed to be tape *sales* became tape *rentals*. If you look carefully, you can still find a few VHS tapes with "$89.99" price tags on them. Consider inflation and how much that was back in 1980!

When you were done with your rental, you brought it back to the store. If they were closed, you dropped it in a "Drop-off Box", which was typically a metal or wooden slot near the shop's front door which would collect the tapes into a bin. Hopefully, if you were courteous, you *rewound* it. That's right: as the movie played, the tape itself would rotate forward. When you reached the end of the film and pressed the stop button, it remained in that position. In an act of courtesy to the next viewer, you pressed the "Rewind" button on your VCR and allowed it a few minutes to spin the tape back to the beginning. This simple act of kindness (later enforced by many stores with a $1 fee for any unwound tape) became a common slogan written on plastic stickers which adorned millions of videotapes: "Be Kind — Rewind!" Parodies of the logo also became common. A cartoon bumblebee with the cheesy pun, "Bee Kind, Please Rewind" became a prominent sticker slapped onto many North American tapes.

    VHS continued to usher in new concepts of motion picture film. Shot-on-video became smarmily known as "Shot-On-Shitteo", referencing the low-budget and often poor quality of a film shot directly onto VHS tape. Straight-to-video was usually a bad sign; often, it meant the film wasn't able to attract a large enough production company to put it in theaters. On the other hand, home video created a large secondary market for film distribution post-theatrical release. Many film house budgets began to skyrocket. Hollywood continued to grow upwards and pump out even bigger and better blockbusters due to the new sales market of home video. Money began exchanging hands on a more rapid level.

It's worth noting that not everyone was a winner. As some might remember, VHS wasn't the first kid on the block. Betamax was technically the first home video format — a smaller and slightly higher quality of magnetic tape introduced in the late 1970s. Although the fight for format dominance continued for quite a while (up to the late 1980s), a good analogy would be the battle between Blu-ray and HD DVD. Although both formats were comparable, in the end, marketing and a few technical aspects were the deciding factor as to which would survive. Many will remember the Beta selection at the local video store getting smaller and smaller as VHS tapes slowly hogged precious shelf space. As one format began to take the lead, consumers (perhaps out of frustration) began to jump ship from Beta. Over time, VHS slowly became the household standard. Some claim it was the availability of pornographic films on VHS which secretly swayed the public, however, most evidence suggests it was more about the availability of home VCR recording. Regardless, if you were amongst the group of consumers who doubled down on Betamax, you eventually ended up on the wrong side of history. These events were best summarized in a joke on an episode of *The Simpsons*. After robbing a house of its video player, the criminal stops mid-stride while running down the street in order to cry out, "Oh no...Beta!"

Regardless of format or device, home video was a game-changer. It ushered in a new entertainment medium for society, with the local mom-and-pop video store being the epicenter of acquisition. It became a reliable go-to for families that wanted to entertain the kids with an afternoon flick. Teenagers would hang out there while pointing out raunchy comedies. It was open late, and it was cheap — a few dollars were all you needed. If you happened to know the clerk, even better. They could give you deals, or even free movies. Heaven forbid you were a straight-up film aficionado. If that were the case, you probably fought for a job there every summer. Many modern-day actors and directors will be the first to tell you just how influential their local video store was in shaping their passion. For some, the idea of pure escapism during a time when there wasn't much to do on a Friday night meant everything.

During its peak decade (around 1987-1997) video rentals sprung up everywhere. It wasn't just the mom-and-pop stores (DIY start-up businesses run by locals in the neighborhood) but convenience stores, general supply stores, supermarkets, and even small-town gas stations that got into the business. Small sectioned-off areas of any store could be lined with various boxes of films on tape. Cottage country would almost always have one large video store off the main road supplying toiletries, bug spray, and VHS. Even a few hardware, grocery, and variety stores expanded to have a corner of the building with a few dozen tapes for the last-minute shopper. While cable TV had films playing all the time, having a movie on tape offered far more ease and convenience. Why wait until Thursday at 2 am to watch your favorite movie on television when you could rent it for a few dollars and watch it at your leisure? The video rental market was booming, and just about every business tried to dip their toes in the water. Mind you, most people were not getting rich, however, local video chains were doing well financially.

Some companies even expanded into renting VHS tapes out of *huge* vending machines. That's right: gigantic, snack-style vending machines which would grab your film choice using a mechanical arm and drop it in the pickup slot, allowing you to rent a tape right there on the spot. While they weren't as common as the latter DVD vending machines of the early 2000s, they did, in fact, exist. With some over eight feet in length, the behemoths had to be moved with a forklift. As you can imagine, they weren't widespread. However, it just goes to show you the far reaches of the video store boom. People wanted to rent flicks, whether they dealt with man or machine. The early 80s models (such as "Video Vendor") could fit a whopping 300 films inside. Eventually, smaller versions were manufactured, albeit with a significantly smaller film selection.

When you have a solid and successful business model going, there's one thing you can count on: competition. When there's enough money changing hands, you can expect a major franchise to form. While many local mom-and-pop stores were coasting into the mid-1990s, various companies and corporations took notice. Eventually, larger conglomerates with stronger financial backing would step into the spotlight. While smaller franchises such as Movie Gallery and Hollywood Video (with Canadian equivalents like Jumbo Video) would establish themselves in pockets throughout North America, they didn't force out smaller mom-and-pop stores. Sure, they were competitors that cut into the market. However, they didn't *dominate*…nor did they price out most local privately-owned shops. Toward the late 1990s, several changes took place that would rock the video rental world and permanently change the way we view films and entertainment altogether.

2. Fall of An Empire

In the mid-to-late 1980s, the home video market was spreading like wildfire and showed little signs of slowing. One ambitious individual that took notice of the industry was Texas-based software supplier and developer Dave Cook, who in the mid-1980s decided to shift out of software development and into video rentals. A bold move. After buying into a franchise called "Video Works" in 1985, he quickly left due to frustrations with their rigid business structure. Having a taste of the market, he decided to open a store of his own which he named "Blockbuster Video Inc". Starting up in Dallas with about 10,000 tapes on the shelf, he soon realized there was a strong demand for the product after he was flooded with customers on opening day.

While many video store owners stepped into the business due to previous experience in film, television or other entertainment mediums, Cook was instead experienced in software and distribution. Combined with his previous knowledge in running a business, things expanded quickly. Soon, one lone Blockbuster became several. After investing in and building a separate warehouse for distribution, Cook found he could open new locations at rapid speed. Not only that, but using his software database experience he could appropriately tailor and distribute tapes to various communities based on specifically targeted demographics. After only two years in the game, Cook had already expanded the franchise to 19 stores.

It's worth mentioning that Blockbuster adhered strictly to a "family-friendly" model, typically in contrast to their competition. This difference played an unexpected role. Mom-and-pop style start-ups usually didn't pander to anyone in particular. You could find family films alongside outlandish pornography, violent thrillers, and just about everything in between. Store clerks could often smoke, joke or just hang out in the back of the store when bored. Don't believe me? Ask any 1980s independent video store employee how stressful their job was. Then listen as they regale you with stories about how relaxed and lackadaisical those days were. Didn't like a customer? Simply tell them off. If you showed up and knew how to work a cash register, you had a job. They could carry and stock just about any film, renting it to whomever they liked. It was mostly no-holds-barred, and stores were unconcerned with strict adherence to any policy or public complaints. It was the Wild West of VHS tape rentals. That is, until Blockbuster Video began popping up in each and every neighborhood.

By 1990, Blockbuster was buying and taking over smaller video franchises. They were on the way to becoming a billion-dollar company, and fast. They were efficient and clean, and they had their staff dress in professional uniforms. They ran a tight ship — all locations were the same with giant blue-and-yellow banners, perfect lighting, and polite employees ready to help in a friendly manner. They offered membership perks and deals constantly and consistently. The floors were mopped, shelves were spiffy and there were no porno flicks to be seen. The new kid was taking over, and their growth was exponential. After a few major corporate mergers, including a 1993 purchase by Viacom for $8.4 billion, Blockbuster expanded their horizons overseas and into the UK. After buying out Ritz Video, Blockbuster became the number one video chain in both America and the United Kingdom. They quickly found themselves decimating the competition. As they hit the mid-1990s, many will remember the smaller mom-and-pop stores closing for good. It was like a hot knife cutting through butter. In only several years, the media rental giant had utterly dominated the market. A few independents stayed afloat due to personal community support. Most folded almost overnight.

Although it's impossible to speak to every former independent mom-and-pop video store owner/employee, it's doubtful you can find one with anything good to say about Blockbuster. Despite "wholesome family entertainment" on the outside, they were well known to industry insiders as being anything but wholesome. The truth is that they were a corporate juggernaut focused on dominating local competition by whatever means necessary. If it meant spying on and ratting out local independents for renting unlicensed films, they did. Employees who made the transition to Blockbuster from failing mom-and-pop stores often didn't last long due to harsher policies and stricter rules. It was a franchised corporate conglomerate, uniform in concept and soulless to most old school video store owners who loved the unique and intimate feel of DIY operations. Nevertheless, Blockbuster continued to steamroll through the industry.

Even "double-taping" didn't hurt the multimedia behemoth. What is that exactly? Since the dawn of the VCR (the device which plays and records VHS tapes), people quickly figured out how to duplicate a film. You could simply "double-tape" a VHS if you had two VCRs. Hook one of the units' OUTPUT into the second one's INPUT and voila! You could now record a copy of whatever you had rented. This surprisingly didn't have much effect on business, probably since the average person only watched any given film once. Only hardcore film fans practiced the trick, already renting and watching movies more than the statistical average. Not only that, but almost all movies on VHS featured a heavy-handed warning about jail time and prosecution should you ever get caught duplicating a film. In reality, nobody was ever seriously convicted or prosecuted. It was more of a fear-based deterrent. For many law-abiding families, it worked. Folks weren't selling VHS copies or "dupes" out of their basement, if for no better reason than the inconvenience and hassle of trying to make money with such a labor-intensive scheme. Unlike DVDs, you couldn't fit a hundred into a gym bag either. VHS were bulky and took up quite a bit of space. Video rentals went relatively unaffected.

There were some minor losses due to local competition, bootleggers, store kiosks and cable television channels. To combat this, Blockbuster began selling other merchandise such as candy and snacks. While this doesn't sound like it would be enough to make a difference, it did, and mostly thanks to children. Apparently, a small mountain of over-priced junk food in front of a cash register is enough to drive little kids into a minor frenzy. If they were about to rent *101 Dalmatians* for the 5th time, they wanted treats to go with it. How much could a video store profit off chocolate bars and snacks alone? According to most former employees, it was more than you might think. A lot more.

A side note worth mentioning: beginning in the mid-to-late 1980s, many midsize video rental stores also rented console video games. Nintendo, Super Nintendo, Sega Genesis, etc. would get their own shelf space. This trend continued with Blockbuster, as they would rent out whatever new gaming system was relevant and in demand, along with those games. Whatever the kids wanted, they did their best to offer it.

Other multimedia formats came and went. As mentioned, Betamax was already dead and buried by the time the 90s hit. CED and Laserdisc were two other video formats that made brief appearances on the market, but we'll get into those later. Spoiler: they never caught on. It wasn't until the introduction of the DVD format that VHS would start to see the writing on the wall.

Digital Versatile Disc (DVD, for short) was a digital optical storage disc, notably capable of much higher quality playback than anything that came before it. Smaller and far more compact, they appeared on the market circa 1996 and immediately grabbed everyone's attention. The price was decent, and the public watched with amazement as more and more of their favorite films were licensed to DVD for distribution. Movies could be divided into chapters for instant viewing, the audio was higher quality, and bonus material was almost always included in some fashion. A huge improvement, leaps and bounds above VHS. Blockbuster (along with remaining independent stores) quickly began stocking them on their shelves. As the demand for the far superior format grew, VHS rentals dwindled. Not immediately mind you, but fast enough that over the next few years it became apparent that VHS had peaked. They had over-stayed their welcome, like an unwanted party guest, and so the great purge began.

In the beginning, video rental stores would find the pros of DVD far outweighed the cons. Yes, they were easily optioned for final-sale (as opposed to rental) due to their low price point. This meant big box and electronics stores could now cut into the market by selling them straight from the manufacturer. Regardless, the public were still renting films. Most folks would simply purchase a few of their favorite films for $25 - $30 on DVD, then casually rent new releases for $3. Although illegal home DVD duplication would become a problem in later years, that wouldn't happen until well into the new millennium. In the late 1990s, most DVD Players would not play pirated or "burned" discs and most computers were too slow to create hundreds of copies in a reasonable amount of time. Eventually flea markets and local video-pirates would exploit duplication effectively, however video stores were relatively safe throughout the 1990s. In the meantime, VHS tapes were slowly being liquidated off shelves and relegated to "For Sale!" bins across the country. What were originally $99 dollar tapes in 1980 were downgraded to 99-cents by 2000. Technology had officially surpassed the format to the point of rendering it obsolete and irrelevant. Just like that. Some mom-and-pop shops would give away tapes, some sold their entire collections in huge lots. Either way, VHS was dying, and DVD was crowned king.

Almost exactly a decade after DVD came out, a sort of big-brother format was released to the public: Blu-ray Disc. As mentioned in the previous chapter, there was a battle between Blu-ray and another format called HD DVD, which Blu-ray won due to several factors (which we'll discuss further in Chapter 10). Out of all physical video formats, Blu-ray was the *final* winner. A crowning achievement in high-definition home video. Just one problem: by the late 2000s, none of that mattered. It was too late. By 2007, a sleeping giant that nobody predicted was about to wake up and stomp the life out of physical rentals forever: online video streaming.

Although the internet had existed as a household service since the mid-to-late 1990s, it certainly didn't resemble the effective highspeed tool it is today. The ability to instantly stream high-quality video didn't come overnight; it took years. Once the public began switching access from phone lines to cable, internet speeds grew faster. Large downloads became more frequent. Entrepreneurs took notice of multimedia rental companies like Blockbuster, along with successful new online shops like Amazon. In 1998, Marc Randolph and Reed Hastings put the two concepts together, creating an online DVD rental service called "Netflix". Although they only had about 900 DVD titles available, they were also Silicon Valley multimillionaires who were able to invest $2.5 million in startup cash. They knew the potential for something big was there. In 1997, Blockbuster was still raking in large gains despite the new market of "online sales". They seemed relatively unphased. One might say, oblivious.

Netflix began on solid ground; however, things didn't boom as predicted. In 1998 they switched from single-pay DVD rentals to monthly subscriptions. This temporarily helped, but by the time the millennium hit, they were officially losing money. 300,000 subscriptions simply weren't enough. In that same year, they offered to sell the company to Blockbuster for $50 million. They didn't bite. Despite this, Netflix wouldn't quit and kept pushing forward. By 2002, Netflix saw a large increase in their subscriptions due to the more affordable price in home DVD players. They continued implementing smart marketing strategies and by 2005 the company had gone public and amassed a catalog of 35,000 films. The tech-savvy film rental company was finally gaining traction and they knew a different ballgame was emerging. They were experienced enough to see that digital video streaming was around the corner, but they weren't quite sure how to utilize it. Originally, they planned to sell a physical "Netflix Box" for home streaming, however, they quickly scrapped the idea after realizing the success of YouTube's web-based streaming. As home internet speed and bandwidth rapidly increased, it was inevitable that someone would offer streaming movies online. In 2007 Netflix introduced a Video on Demand service over the internet. Once again, they started with a small roster of online films and as time passed, they expanded the catalog. Online subscriptions grew as DVD rentals declined. From 2007 to 2011, Netflix grew to nearly 30 million customers. They were on their way to becoming one of the most successful dot-com startups in North America.

Back at Blockbuster Video, online streaming was slowly becoming a death sentence. They failed to latch onto the initial wave of this new platform, now forced to close many stores due to lack of memberships and rentals. If you can imagine Blockbuster holding onto the edge of a cliff, then it was in the year 2010 when their fingers finally slipped. They filed for Chapter 11 bankruptcy and in that year, half of all Blockbusters closed their doors for good. In 2011 all Canadian stores shut down. The company was quickly purchased by Dish Network, and over the next few months, most Blockbuster Video rental stores were shut down forever.

From 2011-2019, what was initially filed down to a handful of Blockbuster stores remaining throughout North America were further pared down to one. Yes, that's right. *One*. As of this writing, there is one lone Blockbuster Video store left in America, privately owned and located in Bend, Oregon. It's highly advisable that if you ever want to experience the thrill of being able to, as the slogan once went, "Make it a Blockbuster night!", then visit that store sooner rather than later. It's literally your last chance.

As for mom-and-pop video stores, they do still exist. Although few and far between, a quick internet search in any major North American city will reveal one or two shops still in operation. Try and do a search in your home state or province. They're completely reliant on neighborhood locals for patronage, as they have been for over 30 years. Most are exclusively rental and sale of DVD and Blu-ray, however many sell other things such as vinyl records, books, magazines, and retro T-shirts. One odd thing you might notice among the films and retro artifacts will be a complete lack of VHS tapes. Usually none! I mean, you would think there would be *some* tapes in an old discount bin next to the Batman T-shirts and Fangoria magazines, right? Probably not. And there is a reason for that.

3. A Perfect Collectible

They say anything can be a collectible. Baseball cards, mint coins, old comics, shoes...shoelaces? What about frying pans? How about Ferraris? If anything can be collected, why are some things more collected than others? Why are some products deemed "worthless junk" while others increase in value? There's a complex answer but we'll try and boil it down to a simple formula. For a thing to be considered a real *collectible*, it typically needs to be:

A. Desired
B. Diversified
C. Scarce
D. Affordable

Follow that guideline and you'll find yourself a real collectible item of some sort. Is a frying pan any of those things? I mean, they're desired and affordable, right? There's probably one lone person out there collecting them, but on average nobody cares. We all have a frying pan, and if not we all know where to buy one. They're not scarce. They're barely diverse. Frying pans are also incredibly boring and not desired for anything other than their utilitarian function. Same with shoelaces. What about Ferrari's? Yes, they're desirable and diverse, but for the average person, they're nowhere near affordable. Sure, some people collect them — insanely rich celebrities, mostly — but they're no longer scarce once you have that kind of money. Nobody thinks of them as collectibles.

Old comic books make a much better example. They fit the description perfectly. Let's see specifically how they can be described. They are:

- Desired. Especially since the rise of Marvel and DC films. New kids coming into the scene want to find the original comics the films are based on. Adults who grew up with them want to go back and recollect issues they lost in their youth. It can be fun searching for them too, because they are...

- Diverse. There exist thousands of different characters, comic lines, artists, variants, and companies. Part of the fun is not only hunting for old comics you desire, but discovering issues that you either forgot about or simply new ones that pique your interest. There are millions of comics in existence. However, some are exceedingly...

- Scarce. Number one issues, rare crossovers, first

appearances, etc. can be very hard to find. Not always, but with so many comics and characters there are bound to be some that some are both desirable and scarce enough to build a collective lust for a specific issue or character. Fortunately, most rare comics are...

- Affordable. Unless you're looking for the top 250 rarest Marvel or DC issues of all time, chances are the average person can afford even pricier issues. Ranging anywhere from $2 - $200, most older comics are technically affordable and usually don't run into the tens of thousands. The average individual can save up and afford that rare first appearance of X, even if it takes a few weeks or months. If desired enough, it's possible.

There is a multitude of different factors working in concert. How people think of a product or item makes all the difference. After all, it's not about any intrinsic or utilitarian function dictating its value but instead a sort of fiat or arbitrary worth created by the collective zeitgeist. What exactly makes a single comic issue worth more than another? What can devalue vs. increase its overall worth? The nuanced specifics within different categories of items will differ, but let's put a pin in that as it will be a focal point of the next chapter. Right now, let's explore some reasons why people would ever want to collect old dusty VHS tapes. I mean, we just established that it's a dead format, right? By and large, those grand old video stores are a thing of the past. They've been relegated to a fleeting memory from the youth of an older generation. So, who cares?

Well, for that specific reason alone, I can guarantee a large portion of VHS collectors do what they do. In other words, the lost memory and retro nostalgia play a huge role in collecting. As we established in the first chapter, people didn't use the video store as a mere tool and function — it was place to hangout, a discovery of art and entertainment. Many youthful memories reside within the now boarded-up windows of former rental stores...and people love reliving those old memories. As digital streaming has allowed us the ease of staying home, it has stolen our physical interaction with a broader community. What used to be an hour-long treasure hunt is now artificially dictated to us using ratings and algorithmic recommendations. What used to be a little-known gem of a motion picture is now a pop culture hit. That last sentence may sound a bit pretentious, but keep in mind what I said before about developing film awareness and taste. Being a film aficionado used to hold a genuine utilitarian function. Nowadays, it's relatively useless. There's far less function and merit to it, as everyone has access to many films, all the time (almost instantly) along with a million reviews/critiques/ratings. Make no mistake, I'm in no way saying this is a bad thing — only that it's far different than how things used to be. Only when you have limitations can you push boundaries, and today there are very few. The limitations of home video used to be a challenge, but it was within those limitations that we built a community. Simply put, there are folks who miss that. Having a personal collection of old tapes that you and your friends can fawn over helps heal the loss of that community. One might say that VHS collectors are those who refuse to relinquish the video store experience altogether, opting to retain and rebuild what is left behind after it collapsed. They're re-animating a lost community and building up a new one from the ruins.

While they'll obviously never regain the number of contributors or participants, it will be a group of people who spend time enjoying a form of lost entertainment within a hub of like-minded individuals. You might expect to see tape swaps, social media groups, websites, documentaries and even books(!) all dedicated to the practice...and that's exactly what has happened.

It's worth pointing out now that within any collector group there are two factions coming together: people who simply enjoy collecting things, and fans of a specific subculture. With VHS tape collectors, we have people who enjoy collecting things who are also fans of cinema. These two groups aren't mutually exclusive so there can be overlap into other subcultures or fandoms on the collector's side, and the same with film enthusiasts who do not collect anything. Quite often, you'll find VHS collectors that display toys, posters, or vinyl records alongside their tape collections. There's something at play here. Call it the "collecting-bug". There exist volumes of books on the topic of collecting which discuss the psychology behind it. As you might imagine, that can be dry and lengthy. Again, the focus of this book is VHS collecting specifically, so forgive me if I avoid the whole psychology of hoarding vs. healthy collecting. For all intents and purposes, we'll assume most VHS collectors are mentally healthy individuals who collect for safe and ordinary reasons. Most often, VHS collecting simply merges hobbyist collectors and fans of films.

Some enjoy collecting due to the "time capsule" factor of aged and forgotten artifacts. In other words, the idea of something physically representing a given time or period. You get to look back in history when browsing through an old antique store or museum. An old 1940's dictionary or perhaps a 1950's Coca-Cola bottle can immediately transport you back to a different day and age in a mere glimpse. Here's the thing: VHS tapes work even better for that. They not only offer retro artwork with the original physical product to hold but an actual motion-picture. You can view into the past, simply by inserting a tape into a VCR and pressing "Play". Watch as Americans smoke cigarettes in an old 1970's restaurant. Giggle as they proceed to ask the waiter for a rotary telephone to be brought out on a plate. See 1960s drag racing, complete with bob-cut high school girls cheering on greasers as they speed down the road in Ford Thunderbirds. You have a front-row seat to glimpse how society was...or, perhaps, how society *presented* itself. What about behind the camera? Can you catch blatant racism in the writing or casting? Are women portrayed differently than in films of today? While you might immediately think of Mickey Rooney's yellow-face stereotype portrayal of an Asian man in *Breakfast at Tiffany's* (1961), many adults are surprised when they look back at *The Monster Squad* (1987) and find it rife with derogatory homophobic slurs. Not to get political — only noting that you may be surprised just how much films from a few decades ago can be aged and dated. We haven't even gotten into laughable 1990s VFX, cringe-worthy monster costumes of the 70s, or the fact that moviegoers were once legitimately frightened by *Abbott And Costello Meet Frankenstein* (1948). When it comes to informing you as to what society was like at any given time, analyzing old cinema can be surprisingly revealing.

For others, it can be a desire to recreate the video store itself. The affordability factor combined with sheer diversification of product is enough to make many people see this as a worthy endeavor. Especially with the near vanishing of all video rental stores; the past decade has encouraged many collectors to not only buy out the stores' tapes but also pieces of the stores themselves. Signs, posters, cardboard cut-outs — even the shelving! That's right, collectors have even bought and stowed away old VHS shelving and racks. A few hardcore fans have recreated entire rental-like displays in their basements and studios, complete with thousands of tapes sprawling the shelves. Do a Google image search on something like "basement video store" and you'll find their dedication to detail is extraordinary. They've effectively recreated the rental stores that are now a mere footnote in history. How's that for a time capsule?

The "thrill of the hunt" is something collectors know all too well, searching through garage sales and flea markets to find that hidden gem or discovering that diamond in the rough after peeling back a filthy blanket in your uncle's basement. There's something exciting about finding obscure treasures for cheap prices. With VHS, it doesn't even have to be a tape everybody is searching for — just something *you* want. A hard-to-find tape from your childhood that isn't worth much to anyone...except you. It's out there, waiting under a pile of self-help tapes at the local thrift store. All you need to do is rummage through that pile of unwanted crap and it's all yours — better hurry!

Some people are just movie fans, and enjoy the fact that VHS is still relatively abundant and cheaper than DVD or Blu-ray. If they've been collecting tapes since their original release in the early 80s, why stop now and make the switch? There's something satisfying about owning the first release of a film. Usually, it's the rare factor coupled with an appreciation for authenticity and originality. The cover art was often elaborate, eye-catching oil paintings, or vintage photography designed to grab the attention of store patrons. Often, in the case of some comedy and horror, they were designed to provoke an emotional response from the passerby...or even offend their sensibilities enough to demand a second look.

While this all makes a strong case for VHS as a collectible item, can we place it within the framework of the previous formula we talked about earlier? Let's see how it holds up. Is it...

Desirable? Oh yes. While not every tape is going to be desired, certain genres, companies, and titles are rabidly sought after. There's something to be said for supply-and-demand, as the prices for rare tapes are only increasing. As we've established, it makes an excellent collectible, even if just for the sheer retro nostalgia. Many people wish to hold part of their film-fandom in their hands, and many folks grew up renting VHS tapes. The video stores, the history, the...smell? Heck, why not? Even the musty plastic and cardboard scent can instantly bring back memories of walking around a Jumbo Video while holding a free bag of popcorn in one hand, a large stack of tapes in the other. They work as both personal time capsules, and as a "rewind" back into how society once was. Small enough to ship in the mail yet big enough to display on the wall. But how varied were the actual films manufactured for the VHS format? Could you describe it as...

Diversified? For sure. In fact, there's far more than you think. There are more movies out on VHS than there are DVD. There's more VHS than Betamax and CED combined. In this sense, VHS reigns as king of home video across the board. There are still many films exclusive to VHS. Seriously. Due to distribution rights and legal issues, there are many movies that simply never went beyond a VHS tape release. This doesn't mean that there's no other way to watch them, but it does mean there's no other way to "own" them. No other way to display it on the shelf. It's hard to even put a number on how many films were released on VHS in North America, let alone across the world. Some films were put out by multiple distributors, leading to some collectors purposely buying a dozen different versions of the same movie. Saying VHS had a diversified film roster would be an understatement. However, if hundreds of millions of tapes were manufactured, aren't they now *overtly* abundant? Can one really consider VHS to be...

Scarce? Yes. More and more each day. It wasn't until the late 1990's/early 2000's when rental stores started liquidating entire inventories. Many were not patient to keep their old merchandise either. Some stores couldn't give tapes away, while others simply threw away their doubles. Much like CD vs. Audio Cassette, the losing format was often viewed as junk. Many tapes were sold to random people for a few dollars. It was eventually regarded as a dead format and many people tossed their old collections in the trash. Those who held onto them often stowed them in the garage or basement. You might not know this, but the magnetic tape inside the plastic shell is very prone to mold. Any water damage or dampness inside a box of VHS and they'll easily develop a mold that can eat right through the tape. Over time, many old VHS have been lost to the tape-hungry fungus. If they're becoming scarcer every day, can you really say that they are considered...

Affordable? Totally. Unless you're buying ultra-rare tapes on eBay, chances are you'll find most VHS still sell for a very low amount. Garage sales, thrift stores, and trade shows will usually sell them between $1 and $2. Even if you're targeting a specific tape on the internet, chances are it's under $40. This is still very affordable, especially compared to many other collectibles on the market. Between the small number of people *wanting* them and a large amount of people being *unaware* of their value, it's still a great time to collect. Even if they do understand that some people collect tapes, they still wouldn't have a clue as to what any single film is worth. Because of this, you can often find them at a steal. Not only that, but old-school tape collectors are often quick to help new folks on the scene, usually providing very fair deals.

While some collectors have literally hoarded VHS since 1978, the majority have only started tape hunting in the past decade or so. It's especially 20 and 30-year-olds who tend to be the ones ramping up the movement. Think about it. Having recently joined the working class, they're now at a point where they can afford to hunt down the forgotten films of their youth. It's hard to collect anything when you're in college or living in a dorm with roommates. Currently, Millennials and Gen-X are the primary collectors in the field. If you think about where Millennials have been situated in the past two decades, it makes perfect sense. They grew up with tapes as a prime source of entertainment throughout their childhood. Then suddenly, VHS vanished. Today, they realize tapes are scarce yet still affordable. You can hunt them down in your spare time and display your trophies to your friends online. Heck, you can even watch them in a VCR!

They're simply a perfect collectible.

4. Adjust Your Tracking

Are all films on VHS worth the same amount in dollars? Certainly not. As stated, some are worth a ton while some are so prevalent they're practically worthless. Many are considered "commons"; not rare yet somewhat desirable. Some genres are shunned altogether. Although this will vary from person to person, there's a general consensus on what certain VHS tapes are worth. In order to try and separate the wheat from the chaff, we need to understand the factors that make some tapes both scarce *and* desirable.

The first thing to say outright (and this is basic knowledge to anyone who collects tapes) is that old horror films are the most valuable, period. No two ways about it. This is the most obvious thing to anyone with any experience collecting VHS. The horror genre is by far the most collected and desired category. Don't believe me? Walk by the tape section at the nearest thrift store, then tell me how many scary movies you see vs. comedy, drama, western or fantasy. Rest assured, it has nothing to do with demonic possessions, evil curses, or "bad mojo". Quite the opposite. Most fans tend to fall on the skeptical side and are not easily frightened. It has everything to do with taboo, curiosity, excitement, thrills, confronting the unknown, etc. We can go on for days, but we don't need an essay on why some people gravitate towards being scared and facing their fears. Nor do we need a diatribe on why youth are attracted to things that pique their excitement. If horror movies are the height of absurd thrills, it's no wonder so many kids gave pause while walking by the "Scary Movie" section at the video store. They're the pinnacle of that primal exhilaration that makes us feel alive and excited. They stimulate a core human emotion that's lost on much of modern society. How often do we feel genuine fear since we left the Serengeti in exchange for suburban sprawl? For the average North American middle-class automaton, not often. Horror films hit on core emotion. At worst, they're the equivalent of slowing down to rubberneck a car crash as you drive by. Actually, at worst, they're filmed so poorly they make you laugh out loud at how the director and cast could be so inept! Regardless, it's the most desired genre many times over.

    If this is the case, then why are they so hard to find today? Is it because they were all scooped up by early-millennium tape poachers? While horror fans *do* tend to be rabid in their means of acquisition, it's not solely that. Remember how Blockbuster Video basically shifted the home video market to a "family-friendly" model? As many of the mom-and-pop independents liquidated their merchandise, much of the more notorious films were simply discarded altogether. The horror films that Blockbuster did carry were usually mainstream productions. Some smaller VHS distribution companies fashioned cover art so controversial that family-oriented stores refused to display it on their shelves. If you look at the artwork from Continental Home Video, Midnight Video, or even Genesis Home Video, you'll find some pretty intense stuff. In the 1980s, those eye-catching covers were part of the reason people rented the movies in the first place. As the 1990s hit, they were denigrated as "too sleazy and gory" by many struggling indie stores. Many were simply sold or tossed out. Fast forward another decade and those that remained on the market were now rare. Horror movie fans (an already nerdy base within the category of film aficionados) would start to view these lost controversial tapes as the rarest of the rare.

It's hard to even get a sense of how many VHS copies of any single film exist. How many of X was manufactured from Y company? Those distribution companies kept very few records. Whatever was left to public record was mostly lost back in the late 1990s. Smaller distributors such as Rae Don Home Video (a company who released insanely bad films — more on them later) operated out of tiny warehouses (Rae Don's was in California). Exactly how many detailed record books could they have kept? Much of what exists today is speculation at best. Some companies are a mystery altogether. Again, more on that in a later chapter; just understand that unlike many comic book companies or other collected artifacts, much of the 80s & 90s tape distribution remains a mystery. Because of that, you never know when a specific tape will simply stop showing up in the second-hand market altogether. There were only so many copies made and eventually some VHS will become next to impossible to find. At least, impossible to find at a decent price!

Does a film being released only on VHS and not Blu-ray or DVD make a difference? Many collectors will state that this is a factor, however, there's not a ton of evidence to back that up. As of writing this, cult horror movies like *The Keep* have yet to have a DVD release (due to licensing issues), however it's not exactly a rare gem. Partly due to its wide VHS distribution, you can still find it at a decent price. Just because you can't find it on DVD doesn't really make a rare treasure. Some may argue this, but it's *typically* not a major signifier of worth. Popularity vs. manufacture plays a more substantial role.

A funny thing has happened over time. You might assume popular movies would be the most desirable tapes to collect, yes? Something like *The Terminator* (1984) was a huge Hollywood hit, right? Many folks cite it as one of their favorite sci-fi/action films of the 80s. You might expect it to be worth a lot in the tape trading market, as opposed to some unknown low-budget indie horror flicks like *The Return of The Alien's Deadly Spawn* (1983). Perhaps you see where I'm going with this. It's *because* of that very reason something like *The Return of The Alien's Deadly Spawn* is worth 100x more. Hit films like *The Terminator* were widely manufactured for the home video market. Not only did everyone want a copy, but most people *still* own a copy. It's not rare. It's super common and easy to find. Something like *The Return of The Alien's Deadly Spawn* has become a rare gem. Not only was it originally scarcely distributed, its gory cover art made it even harder to find, and therefore even more sought after. Make no mistake, it's an entertaining movie, but it's no masterpiece of cinema. It's a shlocky low-budget gory monster movie. However, the point that needs to be understood is simple:

*The VHS most people **DIDN'T** want back then are **NOW** desired today.*

The ones that got thrown away or left in the backroom of the video store covered in dust are now the "rares". Traders and collectors of all sorts of artifacts understand this principle. It's a pretty universal concept within *any* collecting forum. If anything, VHS collectors simply take this philosophy to a more extreme level. The ineptest, shlocky, D-grade, poorly acted, terribly directed, over-the-top ridiculous exploitation films are usually the most sought after and valuable ones on the market.

Another factor to consider when trying to determine the value of any particular tape is the VHS case itself. From the beginning, VHS tapes were manufactured with a few different types of cases: slipcase, book box, clamshell and big box. The casing isn't always the determining factor of worth and value, but it certainly plays a role. Often — and this is a very broad principle — the larger the case, the rarer it is. Partly because many video stores had a bad habit of literally cutting VHS boxes down with scissors in order to fit their rental display cases. These cut-up cases are now referred to as "cut box", and while many folks still collect them, they are considered damaged goods. Think of it like a bent-up comic book with the cover torn in half. At this point, let's shed some light on the specific boxes and cases manufactured for VHS tape:

Slipcase: By far the most common style of VHS packaging. A thin, folded cardboard case designed to perfectly fit a VHS tape which it could slip out of, usually from the bottom. These were around since the beginning and all the way up to the late 2000's when the last tapes were manufactured. The artwork was printed directly onto the cardboard. As time progressed, the quality of cardboard evolved too, becoming thicker and glossier. The colors of many early tapes are often quite faded due to time, quality and sun exposure. Slipcases originally shipped shrink-wrapped in clear plastic. If you find any of them still sealed in the wrapper it can slightly increase the value (depending on the rarity of the film). Despite being the same size as the VHS tape itself, many slipcases were still cut-up in order to fit the hard-plastic shells that video stores used as their own display/rental cases. Most stores did this because it would ensure solid protection when customers would physically mistreat a rental. Unfortunately, this ruined the original box it came in and therefore many collectors will avoid cut boxes when possible.

Book Box: A slightly larger slipcase-style cardboard case, big enough that the cover would fold-open revealing the tape itself. This resembles opening a book, hence the name. MGM/Fox was the major company to manufacturer this style of case. Although there were other companies with similar boxes, most tapes you'll find today utilizing this design are from that company. Some colloquially refer to the smaller dark-blue Fox Home Video cases as "Fox Box", which are almost a cross between slipcase and book box. Some also refer to these as "Sliders" as the VHS slides out from the side as opposed to the bottom. While these aren't super common, they're only slightly more rare than traditional slips. They can still be found cheap, especially non-horror and more mainstream films.

Clamshell: Heavy-duty plastic cases, usually black, which had the artwork printed on paper and then slipped inside a transparent cover. Some companies (such as Video Gems) featured artwork printed onto the plastic case itself. While there was a universal size, it is possible to find different sizes and colors. Typically, these were utilized in the early 1980s and few were produced into the 90s. Most companies eventually switched over to slipcase, as it was cheaper and easier to manufacture. The clamshell cases provided greater protection to the tape and helped them stand out on a store shelf, however, many rental stores still cut them up. Although not as common as slipcase, they're still much more common than the big box format. One of the only major companies to continue using clamshells into the latter era was Walt Disney.

Big Box: The rarest of VHS cases — at least, if they're *intact*. Far too often, video stores were quick to take a pair of scissors to these large cardboard boxes. The inner-plastic trays were frequently thrown away and what was left was a hack-job of a case. On average, they ranged from one to three inches larger than the VHS tape itself. They used strong and thick cardboard with a traditional wax-like coating, prominently displaying the artwork in full view. Inside was a plastic tray to keep the actual tape from moving around. Even most intact boxes are in poor shape today, with most having been tossed around for three decades. Many are faded and crumpled, but with a bit of digging, you can certainly find some in good condition. As you might imagine, not many companies continued to manufacture them after they discovered the extra effort put into producing them was all in vain. In the early 1980s they stood out on the shelf, but over time most were cut up and squashed into plastic rental cases. Once the 1990s hit, their manufacture completely diminished.

There do exist other forms of boxes and cases. These are simply the most common styles you're bound to find. One could argue that rental store "cut-boxes" are the 2nd most commonly found style of case. When many video stores liquidated their inventory in the early 2000s, they dumped thousands of cut boxes into the collector market overnight.

Again, understand that just because a tape was released in big box format does not equate significant monetary value. For example, collectors of rare martial arts movies don't always show much interest in mediocre kung-fu films just because they were put out in big box format. The case itself is secondary when evaluating the overall worth of any specific VHS. The genre, film, and scarcity make so much more of a difference. It's only when we start to compound these individual traits that we begin to see its value and desirability rise. A crappy mainstream drama on big box would typically be worth less than a horror film in slipcase format. Do not let display cases be the determining factor alone.

How much does the physical condition of a case or tape play into its overall value? Not nearly as much as other graded collectibles (i.e. comic books). Expect a price drop if a case is significantly damaged or there is an issue with tape playback. If the damage is minor, it's not a big deal. Small scuffs and stickers are to be expected. Unopened and still-sealed tapes are always great, just don't expect that to double its value or anything unless it's exceptionally rare. Most people don't haggle over small things considering almost all older tapes are previously viewed. Only with rare tapes does the condition significantly affect it's worth.

What about screeners? For those unfamiliar, "screener versions" are the initial demo tapes sent out to various sources before the movie's official home market release. They were shipped to video stores, award shows, and critics — anyone who required an early copy. They would display some sort of watermark during playback telling the viewer they were watching a screener version which was "Not for public display". Or some message explaining that it's not for sale. Are they worth more than official home video releases? Typically, no. There *are* some folks who collect screeners but frankly, they're few and far between. Not every film had a screener version, and most people find the watermarks downright annoying. If it's not a common tape, maybe you can find some demand for it. But for common titles, screeners are not particularly desirable or special.

How about *blanks*? Many have forgotten that blank recordable tapes were a big part of our culture. Purely utilitarian? Yes. However, we would use them to record our favorite TV shows, duplicate a beloved movie rental, or just document our personal lives on video. While they aren't exactly worth a lot, many collectors will tell you it's a good idea to have a few blank tapes handy. They obviously don't manufacture them anymore and they're getting harder to find each year. You might not think of their slipcases as "artistic", but they sure did try to look futuristic. Some have mounted their box art into picture frames, others have celebrated their retro appearance in various blogs. There were hundreds of manufacturers. People will often recognize a logo or trademark when they discover one in a thrift store. *Grab them*! Also, note that many hardcore collectors are all about lost or forgotten pieces of film. That's right, even *privately* recorded home videos are collected by some folks. Creepy? Perhaps. What kind of weirdo wants to sit in a basement and watch some stranger's wedding tape from 1988? To be fair, most collect them for comedic reasons. In other words, for the humor of making fun of a terrible birthday party or lame amusement park trip. There's also the endeavor of documenting old TV commercials that are now impossible to find. That is, until you find an old VHS tape at a thrift store with hours of unedited television footage! Those can be a goldmine for the retro-television enthusiast. Just keep an eye out for blank tapes in general. Especially unopened and sealed blanks. They're not a hot commodity but you never know when you might need one.

The distributor of a tape is something most people don't think much about, however, this plays a major role in VHS collecting. What is it about specific company releases that separate two versions of the exact same film? Assuming the run-time and edit of a film are the same, aren't they both worth the same amount? Nope. Typically, the *original* North American release is the most desirable. Once again, chalk it up to the collecting mentality: the original production run and manufacture of something is usually more desirable to collectors. What people remember seeing on video store shelves also plays a key role. The older the better, as that increases the overall rarity. Also, take into consideration that the quality of tape often varied from company to company. Some distributors were known for having the best transfers and in the highest quality. Other companies cheaped out and would use low-grade transfers on substandard tape. This makes a difference. Some people actually *watch* the films they collect! As we established, most folks collecting VHS are fans of cinema, and films are meant to be watched. Another thing: many distribution companies featured exclusive cover artwork that made them stand out on the shelf. Perhaps it was a trademark border or giant logo. For others, it was unique oil paintings that donned their clamshells. For some, it was horrible crayon-like artwork. In fact, many of those cheap-looking covers are now lusted after, simply due to how hilarious and amateurish the artwork was. Some of it was so inept it bordered on high comedy.

Only when you start to combine all these factors can you start to see why some tapes are worth more than others. Let's go back and take our random example of *Return of The Alien's Deadly Spawn* and see how it fares. We'll specifically go with the 1983 Continental Video release of it. We can describe it as…

- A horror/cult/b-movie
- The original release
- Over-the-top, non-family-friendly cover art
- Big box
- Decent quality transfer
- A fun and entertaining movie

All these traits make it a desirable and sought-after tape. The only thing that keeps it from being super rare is that it was widely manufactured and distributed in the USA. Its distribution to places like Canada was minimal. Finally, as mentioned in the above breakdown, it's a fun and entertaining movie. That contributing factor has been glossed over a fair bit in this chapter, as it should be obvious that collectors want to own cool things. VHS collectors typically collect fun and watchable films. Forgetting the *cool movie* aspect would be a grave mistake. After all, wasn't that the whole point in renting movies in the first place?

5. The Distributors

Consumers bought and rented VHS from the video store. That part, everybody understands. But who did the video stores buy their inventory from? Who was manufacturing and distributing those tapes? If the previous chapter established that distribution companies play a role in determining a tape's value, then what is it about specific distribution labels that have attracted cult-like followings behind them? Most people don't recall much more than the fleeting memory of an old company logo or cover art, and perhaps some colorful insignia adorned to a clamshell case. Most people don't think twice about it. VHS collectors, however, have paid close attention. Over the years, many have come to understand that each distributor tried to curate their own specific line of entertainment. Many companies tried hard to build a respectable filmography. They'd fight for licensing rights to popular movies tooth-and-nail. Well, not all. Some were opportunists, simply looking for low-budget flicks to scoop up when the time (and price) was right. Others didn't care at all, releasing anything and everything, quality be damned. Some specialized in X-rated adult films, others in serious drama pieces. Some tried to do both at once! In the late 1980s, the home video market was exploding. Many video stores would buy anything to fill their shelves. Distribution companies would be there to fill their needs.

      The following is a brief glimpse into the history behind ten of the more popular (and notorious) VHS distribution labels. Hopefully, it helps establish why some specific lines of tapes are desired, however the following needs to be stated: there are folks that simply collect certain VHS distributors due to their box art alone. When you have a row of one style of box with a specific border, it looks uniform on the shelf. For some, that's all they care about. They just look good when displayed together. Nothing wrong with that, but once you understand the history behind some of these companies, it may offer a new perspective on where they came from and why they released the films we love. On the other hand, some of those distributors saw nothing but dollar signs, which produced many of the bad films we remember cringing at.

      Before the home video boom, lousy movies were relegated to playing in cheap local drive-ins. While they still got funded, it wasn't exactly the most profitable endeavor. Once home video hit, it created an entirely new market. With the right connections, luck, or even monetary sacrifice (i.e. forfeiting royalties) you could get your terrible, poorly written and badly acted flick onto video store shelves across North America. While some distribution companies were taking advantage of inept and inexperienced filmmakers, they were also creating a culture of "so-bad-it's-good" entertainment.

The following are 10 VHS distributors which many collectors will agree are some of the more popular lines of home video; however, please note that this is 10 out of 1,000. Seriously. You could easily write an entire book documenting just half of those companies. Countless distributors have existed, so many have vanished. Much of this history is lost to time. It's hard to even dig up information on popular ones, let alone the obscure ones. Regardless, let's give it a shot:

PARAGON
Operating out of Las Vegas, Nevada, Paragon was one of the earliest VHS companies in the USA to pack a solid wallop when it came to releasing horror and thrillers. While only in business from 1981 to 1985, they were certainly prolific and offered dozens of non-public domain films. Many of their releases were recorded in high-quality SP mode, as opposed to the

cheaper EP mode often used by budget companies. Although their print transfers weren't always the best, they did have a large roster of uncut versions to many of their films. Paragon also became well known for splicing in about 10-15 minutes of trailers and previews before the feature film itself - a trend that eventually caught on throughout the entire home video market. Starting out as "King of Video" (with direct ties to Cannon Films), they quickly dropped that name and changed over to Paragon Video Productions where they regularly released dozens of movies on tape. Spanning multiple genres, it's fair to say they often focused on horror and exploitation of the 1970s. It's also worth mentioning their box art, which was usually the film's theatrical poster, along with their logo (which took up the bottom 1/5th of the box). While most of their films came in slipcase, they did put out quite a bit of big box. Not much is known about the demise of the company, but their film catalog speaks for itself and is definitely sought out due to uncut versions of many of their films.

ASTRAL
A highly sought-after roster of Canadian tapes, Astral Video was known for their large plastic clamshell cases, minimalist film synopses and iconic blue-rooster-in-space logo. Eventually they would switch over to regular slipcases, however, their early large

blue-bordered clamshell cases are now a rarity (along with their white cardboard slipcases). Astral itself began in 1973 as a chain of photography concessions inside Miracle Mart stores throughout Quebec. Owned by Harold Greenberg and his brothers, they quickly expanded into Angreen Photo and then to Astral Photo. Eventually, they acquired a motion picture lab, and in 1983 began duplicating and distributing high-quality VHS. They also gained success shifting between movie distribution and large-scale film investments. They expanded even further into buying entire television networks, and finally ditched VHS altogether in 1996. By 2000 they had amassed themselves into the multimedia giant "Astral Media", and after purchasing multiple broadcasting companies they were finally bought out for $3 billion by Bell Media in 2012. Behind each Astral VHS tape lies the ambitious success story of the Greenberg family and their rise to power in North America. They effectively created a multimedia empire. And here you probably just thought they had a funny logo, didn't you?

WIZARD
One of the original big box genre labels, Wizard Video began in early 1980. Film and home video mogul Charles Band had already created MEDA Home Entertainment (later becoming "MEDIA"), and with

this experience, he channeled his fondness for horror and European B-movies into its own label, "Wizard". It began with slipcase releases, however, to stand out on the store shelf, they quickly switched over to big box format and implemented lurid cover art to catch the eye of video store patrons. It worked. Titles like *Zombie*, *Headless Eyes*, and *Crimson* caught the attention of many fans and are now highly sought after. They released dozens of big box videos but eventually called it quits when they realized stores had begun chopping down the boxes to save shelf space. Originals are highly in demand. As a side note, in 2013 Charles Band began selling original 80s big boxes that were said to have been found in storage. Cue in controversy as some hardcore collectors have put them under the microscope and called foul, claiming that they're manufactured duplicates. Whatever the case, Wizard Video will always remain a fan favorite, with Charles Band being one of the pioneers of North American home video.

VIDEO GEMS

From the 1980s to roughly 1990, Video Gems were most notable for putting out bizarre 1970s exploitation films with some of the biggest clamshell VHS cases around. A California-based company (although they had a division of sorts in the UK), many of their VHS cases were a mixture of cardboard and plastic, featuring both boxes and oversized clamshells. Often the artwork was literally printed onto the plastic itself! Like many distributors, their catalog consisted of multiple genres, however, they tended to primarily focus on releasing films of the 1970s. With titles like *The Severed Arm*, *The House of Seven Corpses*, and *I Dismember Mama* they quickly gained the attention of horror fans everywhere. At the same time, their roster also expanded out to westerns (*Cain's Cutthroats*), comedies (*Boob Tube*), dramas (*Black Starlet*) and the just-plain-weird (*Octaman*). They also touched upon some of the odd titles from the 1960s such as *The Slime People* and *The Human Vapor*, many of which were difficult to find elsewhere. With a diverse catalog coupled with unique packaging, Video Gems are still very collectible and sought after. Many can still be found on the aftermarket, albeit far more scarcely than Warner clamshells or most other US companies who put out a similar style of clamshell tapes.

CONTINENTAL

Hailed by some as King of The Big Box, Continental was responsible for putting out a few dozen of the sleazier B-movie flicks from 1984 to 1987. Operating out of Los Angeles, to this date they still hold claim to having put out some of the more visceral and in-your-face VHS cover art ever produced. Much of their film roster (including manufacturing a few tapes under their sub-label "Comet") was released in huge eye-catching big box format. Also notable is the fact that they occasionally released "double features" — two films on one VHS tape which played back-to-back. In the VHS rental days, that was a huge bonus. Coupled with their low selling price of $29 - $39 per film, they were certainly well received by fans of shlock cinema. For whatever reason, it wasn't enough to keep Continental going and thus, their time on the market was brief. Towards the late 80s, they switched over to a regular slipcase format, but it's their big box releases that many collectors lust after. Finding them in good condition is tough but certainly worth the hunt.

VCII
Sister-label to the adult-film oriented distributor VCX, VCII Incorporated (not to be confused with "VCI" or "VEC") were based out of Burbank, California and operated from 1980 to 1992. Although they were technically in operation for roughly a decade, their actual releases were rather sporadic. With a "Film Classics" menu alongside a big box horror selection, you might say they were diverse yet almost random in their genre choices. Most suspect that VCII was merely VCX dipping their toes into more low-budget films while operating the adult film company as their

cash-cow. If random film distribution rights came their way at the right price, they scooped it up. Regardless of motives, VCII at least covered all the right bases, putting out both slipcase and big box formats for many of the same films. A bold move for the company, almost as bold as their logo occasionally taking up 1/3rd of the box art itself! Fans fondly remember them for shedding light on horror oddities such as *The Prowler*, *Mardi Gras Massacre*, and *Night of The Demon* — many of which are now highly sought after in the big box collectors market.

INTERGLOBAL

The dynamic, but doomed, Canadian VHS distributor, Interglobal Home Video was founded in Toronto, Ontario in 1984. Known for their iconic bordered slipcases with often exclusive artwork, they first began by releasing classic B&W and public domain films. Their affordable EP and LP mode tapes quickly saturated Canadian and US shelves alike. Shortly after, they expanded their catalog to include movies of the 1960s and 1970s, many of which they had exclusive distribution rights to. They rode the VHS gravy train throughout the mid-1980s, even adding newer flicks such as The Boogeyman and The Tomb. While the quality of their tape transfers was regarded as decent, some of their releases suffered an unacceptable glitch: the endings to some films cut off early. This was obviously not tolerated by renters, and store owners began to take notice. By 1987 their market share began to suffer. Much of their catalog was now available from other companies, and often in superior quality. By 1988 they were falling victim to bigger and better distributors and finally closed for good in 1989. Although many renters may remember Interglobal with a sour taste in their mouths, they did offer obscure films at an affordable price. Oddball flicks such as *Ghosts That Still Walk*, *Legend of The Werewolf*, and *Long Weekend* kept them on horror fans' radars, and still to this day you can easily spot rows of Interglobal tapes on collectors' shelves.

GENESIS
The US-based Genesis Home Video was certainly not one of the more prolific, nor respected VHS distributors. They were well known for putting out poor quality, sometimes barely watchable, transfers. Even in SP mode, they were not up to par. Beginning sometime around 1980 and clearing out around 1986, little info about the company remains. They released mostly horror along with a few random dramas and thrillers. However, points off for throwing in a lot of public domain pieces. On the other hand, they had a handful of exclusives, but more points off for poor quality transfers. One thing they were known for, in a good light, was *epic* horror cover art. This was

certainly a case where the company used flashy paintings and photography in order to sell a flick that paled in comparison to its box art. Movies like *Night of Horror* and *Revenge of the Zombie* may have looked terrifying on the video store shelf, however halfway into the film and most viewers were rolling their eyes (if not completely falling asleep). Their films were released exclusively in slipcases — their 1980's synthwave-looking logo and brand of "Next Wave in Entertainment" was, in retrospect, rather misleading. Most of their tapes can be found relatively cheap, although a few are valuable. Some have jokingly dubbed them the "Vaporwave of VHS" and with their distribution tactics, low-fi quality, and overall presentation it's easy to see why. Still, hats off to their in-house graphic designer; they did an amazing job.

MIDNIGHT VIDEO

Based out of Los Angeles, California, the notorious Midnight Video only released eight films during their brief stint on the VHS market — but they went straight for the jugular. All eight films were released in large big box format, and all eight were bloody as they come (both in regard to the films *and* their cover art). They were, in fact, a sub-label for the adult video distributor Wonderful World of Video, also released under the label "Select-A-Tape". Four of their films were from Andy Milligan (*Bloodthirsty Butchers*, *Torture Dungeon*, *The Man with Two Heads*, *The Rats Are Coming! The Werewolves Are Here!*) and three were from H.G Lewis (*Gruesome Twosome*, *Wizard of Gore*, *The Gore Gore Girls*). The eighth and final one was the notorious horror/comedy *Microwave Massacre*. Although short-lived, Midnight Video remains one of the more collectible VHS distributors due to its scarcity, short roster, big box format, dark artwork, and sheer notoriety. All eight tapes were adorned with large colorful paintings, surrounded by a colored border with the Midnight Video top-hat-skeleton logo. They're hard to miss and stand out on a shelf like no other.

RAE DON

Operating out of a small warehouse in Southern California, Rae Don Home Video is responsible for distributing some of the best-worst films in US history. As the 1980s video store concept ramped up, Rae Don was there to release the awkward low-budget films that no other company would touch. Their catalog defined bottom-of-the-barrel. The directors were inept. The camerawork poor, and the acting non-existent. Actors screwed up their lines on screen with cringe-worthy dialogue. Their reputation was that of a company who would release anything — proven by what many consider their crowning achievement: *Alien Private Eye* (1989). While some consider Troma to be the king of crap, Rae Don takes things one step further as they were somehow *less* self-aware. They bought many of their films from third-party companies, slapped quick artwork onto a slipcase and then hocked them to as many video stores as they could. They weren't bad on purpose. They were just bad. Eventually, video store owners became aware of the poor quality of Rae Don's catalog, and demand for their releases plummeted. Rae Don filed for bankruptcy in 1991, and so was the end to their era. Some of their titles turned up unauthorized on the MNTEX label. Many of the filmmakers weren't paid. Ironically, thirty years later and Rae Don VHS are *highly* sought out and hailed as some of the best-worst films of the 1980s.

There you have it. Just a small taste of the VHS distribution companies that have existed in North America. A thousand VHS tape companies have come into existence since 1978. Maybe more. That's the problem: very little was ever officially documented. In fact, some distribution companies are still a mystery. Take "NEON VIDEO" for example. The company was based in...unknown. They released their films during...unknown. Owned and operated by...unknown.

Yet, you can still find their clamshell (and sometimes slipcase) tapes going for quite a price on the collector market. It's a real conundrum. All we can say is that it was *probably* a US-based company due to a US legal warning on some of the tapes. Even *that* is still technically an assumption because it doesn't list a location of origin or manufacture. Some speculate they were producing tapes illegally without licensing and simply slipped by the radar throughout the home video boom. Who knows? Unless somebody can track down the former owner, it will remain a VHS mystery.

For those making a proactive attempt to document *which* companies released *what*, try the following: IMDB Pro, VHScollector.com, and various VHS "Checklists" that exist in both digital and physical production. Again, this is not an easy feat and you'd be surprised at the amount of missing and unknown information. Even after exhausting all the above historical resources, there is still much unknown. To make things even more difficult, you also need to know the alternate titles to the films in question. Movies were often released under different names by different companies.

Other VHS distributors either moved away from selling tapes or were simply swallowed up by larger companies. Take MEDA, for example. A frontier label started in 1978 by Charles Band, which he named after his wife, Meda. After a slew of VHS and Beta releases, he changed the name of the company to MEDIA due to many people thinking "Meda" was a typo. Around 1984, MEDIA was bought by Heron Communications, who ran it for several years before selling the catalog to Video Treasures. Unfortunately, Video Treasures cheaped out by releasing many of those same films on lesser quality EP/LP transfers. After merging with Anchor Bay, they finally sold their licensing rights to them in 1996. This was not a bad thing, as Anchor Bay was known for putting out premium quality widescreen special editions. After several post-millennium mergers and acquisitions, Anchor Bay was then bought out by Lionsgate where it currently resides. At this point, it's not even close to the initial VHS/Beta distribution company that it began as. Although Lionsgate has put out and distributed many excellent films, its present-day incarnation is more of a multimedia conglomerate. Much like how Astral Video was eventually assimilated into Bell Media, Lionsgate is currently rumored to be in a bidding war featuring the corporate behemoths Amazon, Comcast, and Viacom.

    I wonder if anyone currently owns the rights to Rae Don or Genesis? It's a mystery I'll let you solve on your own.

6. America's Most Wanted

This chapter will need to be prefaced with a heaping amount of warnings and justifications. Some old-guard VHS collectors could be disgruntled by a book openly name-dropping tapes that are of value. Well, guess what?

1. Just because this book lists a tape at a general value doesn't mean it's worth that amount. We're generalizing. A tape is worth what someone will pay for it. Period. Even then, prices fluctuate. Some tapes will unexpectedly increase in value. Others might not sell at all. Really, this is more of a guideline as to what's specifically of interest at the time of writing. Heck, just to be safe, let's limit this list to only 25 tapes. Sound fair?

2. Thrift store and pawnshop managers are *already* checking eBay Sold listings. This isn't new and has been happening for years, especially since the advent of smartphones. They can quickly find out what has sold and for what price. An obscure and lengthy book pales in comparison to the information and tools that most second-hand sellers already possess.

3. If you're an old school collector, you probably have a few of the VHS listed here already. Even if your worst nightmare occurs (this book becomes a best-seller and people across the country start hoarding tapes!) you're now the owner of super valuable stuff. Congrats! Their monetary worth has skyrocketed. Seriously though, if you're ahead of the curve then you're ahead of the curve. However, let's be real: this crazy scenario will never occur, anyway. So, relax!

4. A viral blog or Instagram post will have much more of an effect on prices within the collecting world. VHS tape collectors who are posting pictures and bragging about rare acquisitions on social media will spur on *far* more tape-lust than any nerdy book ever could.

      Another thing: if you happen to have a lot of money and think hunting down the following tapes is now your life goal, simply because some book claimed they're rare and valuable... you're broken. Come on. Simply owning tapes for bragging rights is NOT a healthy practice. These are just movies to keep an eye out for. Perhaps one or two of these you rented as a kid, and now you're inspired to hunt them down. Okay, cool. Unless you're a rabid horror hound who grew up on a steady diet of bad 80's trash, you probably never rented any of these specific releases. Spend that money on another Rolex. Give that trophy wife a 3rd nose job. Have at it. Showing off to a bunch of tape hoarders is pointless.

Finally: To the that one reader who is literally a thrift store owner, now planning to put every obscure VHS behind glass for $49.99 — don't be a fool. No one will pay that. Just put your tapes out for $1 – $2 dollars each. Stop trying to pinch every penny out of your, ahem...donations.

This chapter exists as a means of documentation and observation. If we want to celebrate the lost culture of video stores and VHS, we need to shed some light on what's valuable and — more importantly — *why*.

The following tapes are widely acknowledged as some of the more desired VHS, at least as far as demand vs. selling price. It's entirely possible for someone to pay an absurd amount of money for something lesser known, however, these are pretty much guaranteed to go for some of the highest prices *consistently*. In other words, they're well recognized as both super rare AND desirable within the world of tape collecting. Let's start off with the top three, then work our way to 25:

1. *Tales from the QuadeaD Zone* (1987)
Distributor: Erry Vision Film Co.
Format: Slipcase

Typically, this is #1 in collector circles. Perhaps the most infamous straight-to-video VHS ever released. Written, produced and directed by Chester Novell Turner, this late-80's blaxploitation horror anthology was given a super-limited release of around 100 copies, mostly distributed by the director himself. An ultra-low-budget and ridiculous flick, it's not cliché to tell you that it truly needs to be seen to be believed. *Really*. A shot-on-video masterpiece of Grade-Z cinema, *Tales from The QuadeaD Zone* is not only one of the rarer VHS in existence but also one of the most notorious. The majority of original copies have been lost to time, however, those that still exist will fetch anywhere from $1,000 – $2,000 USD.

2. *Black Devil Doll from Hell* (1984)
Distributor: Hollywood Home Theatre
Format: Clamshell

If one Chester Novell Turner film wasn't enough, his *Black Devil Doll from Hell* comes in at second place. And for pretty much the same reasons as #1. You can already tell from the title of his directorial début that it's a blaxploitation horror flick about a haunted doll. Enough said. It's just as bad and equally as disastrous. Not quite as rare, simply due to the fact that it was given a wider distribution from Hollywood Home Theatre. Regardless, it's super hard to find, utterly egregious, and lusted after by tapeheads across North America. Original VHS copies have sold for anywhere from $700 – $1,000 USD.

3. *The Texas Chainsaw Massacre* (1974)
Distributor: Astral Video
Format: Clamshell

An early Canadian VHS clamshell release of the iconic Tobe Hooper horror classic. You know the film. If not, the name spells it all out for you: a group of youths run astray on a farm, soon running for their lives from a masked cannibal with a chainsaw. Astral Video was a professional company known for putting out high-quality VHS transfers, and much of their catalog is now considered valuable. Why this film and version in particular? Consider it a mixture of vintage distributor meets epic horror, packaged into one heavily fawned-over and rare item. Highly sought after, it regularly sells for $500 – $700 USD.

The next three might be even rarer. However, they are slightly lesser-known and therefore have less focus put on them. Not quite as lusted after, but many collectors still know what they're worth: around $300 – $500, give or take. Can you find them for less? Technically you could find them for 10 cents at a flea market. But chances are you won't. These numbers are simply what they *could* go for in certain circles. They're ultra-rare and many tape hoarders would give their eye teeth for a mint copy. In fact, you'll probably never even *see* one unless you know the right person:

4. *Last House on Dead End Street* (1973)
Distributor: Marquis Video
Format: Slipcase

5. *Just Before Dawn* (1981)
Distributor: Vogue Video
Format: Clamshell

6. *Holy Terror* (1976)
Distributor: Astral Video
Format: Clamshell

You might have noticed: all three of those are from Canadian distributors. That's no coincidence. It seems most Canadian VHS releases ended up being somewhat scarce throughout the USA. Hardcore

American horror fans ended up renting and later hunting down those specific releases. The thing is, since Canadian tapes were less widely distributed, many became rarities to collectors. That certainly isn't a hard rule, and again is a generalization. Just because a horror film was put out by a Canadian company does not equate significant value. Regardless, if you happen to find an old horror VHS tape put out by a Canadian company, you might think twice before tossing it back into Grandma's garage sale bin. A surprising amount of them are desired by both American and European collectors.

Although we've noted that this book is focusing on North American releases, we should ask the question about foreign/overseas VHS: are they as sought after by North American collectors? Well, not so much. The main reason is that much of Europe manufactured their VHS in a different format called "PAL". In North America, it was "NTSC". This variation in manufacturing had to do with the technical processing signal, and thus the two formats are incompatible. You cannot play PAL tapes in a standard North American VCR. Most tapes made in Japan were NTSC, though they often used completely different cover art with subtitles. Unless you have a specific desire for Japanese tapes, most collectors only tend to grab them if the price is right. Some people certainly do collect foreign tapes, but it's simply not as common.

Oh, and yes, for the folks who haven't been paying attention: *yes*, the VHS distributor matters! Something like *Halloween* on MEDA is worth a lot more than *Halloween* put out by Anchor Bay.

The next 19 tapes listed are sought after, most of which you could expect to go from anywhere between $100 – $250 USD. They're desired by many collectors and most will instantly recognize the titles. Some were manufactured more than others, however for different reasons they're all in demand and sell pretty quickly on the collector market.

Let's keep a unique mix of distribution companies just to make it more interesting (but no less honest)...

7. *Video Violence* (1987) - Camp Video - Slipcase
8. *The Prowler* (1981) - VCII - Big Box
9. *Lunch Meat* (1987) - Tapeworm - Slipcase
10. *Screams of a Winter Night* (1979) - VCI - Slipcase
11. *The Microwave Massacre* (1983) - Midnight Video - Big Box
12. *The Demons* (1984) - Unicorn Video - Clamshell
13. *Halloween* (1978) - MEDA - Slipcase
14. *Nightmare* (1982) - Planet Video - Big Box

15. *Return of the Alien's Deadly Spawn* (1983) - Continental - Big Box
16. *The Texas Chainsaw Massacre* (1974) - Wizard Video - Slipcase
17. *The Video Dead* (1987) - Embassy - Slipcase
18. *Dark Night of the Scarecrow* (1981) - Key Video - Slipcase
19. *Halloween Night* (1988) - Atlas Entertainment - Slipcase
20. *Woodchipper Massacre* (1989) - Donna Michelle - Slipcase
21. *Sledgehammer* (1983) - World Video - Clamshell
22. *Frozen Terror* (1986) - Lightning Video - Slipcase
23. *555* (1988) - Slaughterhouse Entertainment - Slipcase
24. *Alien Private Eye* (1987) - Rae Don - Slipcase
25. *7 Doors of Death* (1981) - Thriller Video - Big Box

There you have it, 25 highly desired tapes. There easily exist *thousands* of VHS tapes that sell for significantly high prices. Again, this is just a rough guideline as to a *few* of the more sought-after tapes. That's it! Just some examples. These are merely VHS that are frequently found on many collectors' top shelves. No hard rules. In fact, this should *not* be your top picks. You should have your own!

The primary reason for this chapter existing is to step back and look at the metadata: take note that the catalog listed here is mostly horror movies released between 1978 – 1988. These films were *not* cherry-picked for that timeline or genre. Hopefully, this analysis coupled with the information in the previous chapters can help illustrate *why* these films are so highly sought after. It's a compounding of variables that all lead to a demand for a specific film from a certain timeframe. Much of the cover art was controversial. Many of the films were slammed by critics yet hailed by B-movie fans. All released around the development and formation of independent video stores. Many tapes were taken off shelves or lost to time after Blockbuster took over much of the market. Starting to see that pattern I mentioned in previous chapters?

Let's try the opposite: the following are the top three most *commonly* found and *unwanted* tapes. It's unknown if these were technically the most manufactured VHS or not, however, these three are the most frequently found tapes you'll discover while hunting. Don't believe me? Just ask around. Better yet, hit up a thrift store or flea market yourself and prove it to yourself. These are the scourge of VHS collectors and tapeheads everywhere. It's true that they're good films. They were all smash hits. The thing is, they are demonstrably unwanted VHS tapes. So many of these tapes exist you could use them to build a ladder to the moon.

1. *Titanic* (1997)
Distributor: Paramount/FOX
Format: Two-Tape Slipcase

2. *Jerry Maguire* (1996)
Distributor: Tristar
Format: Slipcase

3. *Speed* (1994)
Distributor: Twentieth Century Fox
Format: Slipcase

Notice something interesting? A pattern? Entirely opposite qualities of the most desired tapes by collectors? 1994 – 1997. Family-friendly. Nearly peak VHS production and manufacture. Smash hit Hollywood films. Slipcases. All high on drama and feature attractive actors on the front covers. The subconscious template that many VHS collectors follow (and even non-collectors who choose to either donate rather than keep a tape) should now be obvious.

Other than old grainy horror films, are there other genres or types of movies that are worth anything? Of course, just understand that they're usually from the same desirable timeframe, only sliding more into the realm of cult flicks and B-movies. FYI, "cult" films are simply movies with a cult-like following, often blurring the lines between different genres. And by "B-movie" we mean a movie that's very low budget and not well recognized or received. In other words, think of difficult to categorize films with some semblance of notoriety or controversy. Some early VHS releases of John Waters' films are now quite sought after. Bizarre and outlandish movies like *Mr. No Legs* (1978) and *Begotten* (1990) are also highly desired in their original VHS releases. Again, these are just a few examples. There are hundreds!

What about older films with ultra-obsessive fan bases such as *Star Wars* (1977)? Well, it's a mixed bag. Sometimes, you can find those VHS selling for a lot, however, those tapes were so widely manufactured that it's *highly* questionable when they do. To be perfectly blunt, it seems that many oblivious fans are tricked into thinking a common tape is rare. Movies like *Star Wars* were so widely distributed on VHS that in theory there should be more than enough copies to go around 10x over (regardless of which case, cover or version you're searching for). Still, the odd fan will mistakenly overpay on eBay and then suddenly others think it's a rare gem. It's almost always *not*. When it comes to big-name films, keep an eye out and you're almost guaranteed to eventually find a copy in the wild.

Finally, there's one last point to address within the topic of valuable tapes, and it's an annoying one: The Disney Black Diamond Fiasco.

Around 2016, several internet blogs reported that a specific line of old Walt Disney VHS tapes was now worth a lot to collectors. Like, *thousands* of dollars. Those tapes were "Black Diamond" — a popular line of Disney VHS that featured a small black diamond-shaped logo on the cover. Spoiler: It was all a sham. It's unknown who first made this claim and why. Some say it was a joke. Most say that it was inept bloggers who had the misconception that just because something was *listed* at a certain price on eBay meant that it *sold* for that same price. Sorry, it does not. You can list pocket lint on eBay for a million dollars. That doesn't mean it will sell for that price, or at all. Unfortunately, once one popular blog claimed them to be valuable, many others blindly followed suit. Like force-multipliers, the more blogs that repeated it, the more legitimate it seemed. If you look at eBay sold listings for Disney tapes, it will occasionally show a tape listed for thousands of dollars but sold as "Best Offer Accepted". Basically, this means it *could* have sold for $2. In fact, that's usually the case. Are Walt Disney tapes super rare and worth a lot of money? No, and you can prove it yourself. Drive to the nearest thrift store in any major city and you'll find dozens of children's films. You're almost always guaranteed to find some Black Diamond or Disney "rares" for $2 apiece. This is because they are *not* rare. They are not super valuable. They're common, worth maybe $4 – $5 *max*. You probably even own one and don't even know it.

7. The Good, The Bad & The Unwatchable

By now, you should understand that "bad" or initially unwanted films on VHS are often considered valuable. But what *exactly* is it about bad cinema that so many collectors love? If a film is terribly acted, poorly directed and overall cheesy trash, why even give it a second glance? You probably also understand the basic philosophy behind collecting rare items: the things everyone collectively threw away in their youth are now valuable. Also, understand that re-issues with "Collector's Edition!" scrawled across them are usually not so desirable. You can't design something to be a rare collectible in the same way you can't force an online video to go viral. It's either in demand or it's not. You can't force that. Make no mistake: telling consumers that a VHS is a special collector's edition doesn't make it undesirable. However, collectors don't like to be spoon-fed. Post-millennium high-quality tape releases are great for watching, but that's about it. If that's the goal, why not just watch a Blu-ray? VHS collectors obviously have a retro-infatuation with their memories of tape, especially the mediocre quality. Picture grain and static are a part of reliving the memory. The low budget aspects of the platform are part of the nostalgia, as is the memory of watching a film so bad that you can't help but laugh or cry. That's something that occurred to almost everyone while renting tapes. You watched bad films. Like death and taxes, it was inevitable. You never knew exactly what you were going to get inside a plastic rental case... and sometimes your luck ran out. However, not all hope was lost — if you had some snarky friends, sloppy snacks and enough drinks, you could make it a fun and hilarious night.

Before we dive into the wonderful world of crap, it's worth taking the time to establish what we mean by "bad" movies and the different types of bad films. In fact, let's break things down into 5 different categories, just to sort out any confusion:

1. Cheesy Flicks
Ever seen a movie that was fun, over-the-top, yet not quite up to par? Maybe something that had action and thrills but was poorly directed. Maybe the lead was overacting, or the editing was sloppy. Perhaps the plot fizzled out halfway through and it slowly transitioned from a serious film, to balls-to-the-wall ridiculous. Many action films of the 1980's fall into this category. They aren't terrible — in fact, people may even claim some of them to be their favorite films. They were

wacky and great on a rainy day. The kind of films your family might shake their heads at yet watch to completion. Cheesy flicks were common on VHS. During the video boom, many companies simply threw money at various directors and pumped out fun-but-flawed films to fill video store shelves. Screwball comedies (sometimes questionable in their humor), low budget monster flicks and implausible action films often fell victim to the cheese-factor. They have a ton of heart, but just don't pass muster. The director and cast seem to genuinely care and want to make a decent film. On a scale, they're more good than bad, falling somewhere between entertaining and silly.

2. Bad Movies
This is the most often used expression when talking about films that are so bad yet *still* watchable because of how over-the-top hilarious or lame they are. They cross the line, tipping the scales into the more-bad-than-good territory. The directing, plot and acting are all subpar, with the only redeeming factor being how humorous it all is. There's often a unique level of comedy when someone tries their hardest to create a piece of art, but fails miserably. Think of that one person at the party who thinks they have the greatest dance moves ever, yet in reality, they look like they're having a seizure. Now imagine while they're dancing, they split their pants. You can't look away, and soon

begin laughing at how ridiculous it all is. Actors flubbing their lines. Plotlines that go nowhere. Dialogue that makes you face-palm. It's all waiting for you in the wonderful world of bad movies. Other phrases you might hear used are "Good-bad films" or "Best-worst films". All pretty much describing the same thing: movies that are so bad they're enjoyable. There is a reason why *Elvira* and *Mystery Science Theater 3000* often made fun of them throughout their releases: they provide a ton of hilarious fodder.

3. Shlock Cinema

Once the video boom of the late 1980s and early 1990s hit, a few directors and producers realized that some people (including themselves) enjoyed those bad films. Sometimes, people would even rent them more than once, simply to show their friends and family as a gag. They took inspiration and began to produce those bad flicks on purpose, knowing full well that folks (especially young people) would rent them in hopes of watching something truly silly and ridiculous. This ushered in a whole new subgenre. Yes, bad-on-purpose films did exist before home video and VHS tape. However, they were relegated to late-night drive-ins and grindhouse cinemas, and therefore not quite as common. With the dawn of home video, the market expanded to where kids and teenagers could now slip any VHS tape into the rental stack on the way out of the video store, finally able to watch the bizarre and outlandish films they had only heard rumors of. Writers would pen featherbrained dialogue combined with silly plots that were downright preposterous, and fans would eat up those "shlockbusters" like a trashcan on garbage day.

4. Shot-On-Shitteo
Although fans can argue that "shot-on-video" was merely the *medium* that certain movies were filmed on, it's worth noting that many of those early "SOV" movies were a distinct form of stank. Most simply stunk. Shot-on-video is self-explanatory — movies filmed on magnetic tape, produced specifically for the home video market. As you can imagine, this was often due to budgetary reasons. That should be a red flag right there. This was the video boom at its most economically dubious. Films were put out fast and cheap, with cut-rate directors leading the charge. You shouldn't need to have the colloquial phrase "shot-on-shitteo" explained to you at this point. You get the gist. Many 1980s horror and action flicks adopted this trend, and overtime SOV began to develop a notorious lackluster style. Even the box art was generally compromised. As you can imagine, many VHS collectors have specified in hunting down lost SOV flicks both for the gimmick of being shot on video, and for their atrocious quality. We won't dive too

much into SOV in this chapter. Just be aware that they exist and are often, as the kids say, crap-tastic.

5. The Unwatchable

First of all, the average movie-goer has simply *not* seen many "unwatchable" films. No, just because you hated *Batman & Robin* (1997) or thought *Waterworld* (1995) was lame doesn't make them unwatchable. Some mainstream Hollywood films might fall into the realm of mediocrity, sure. Even "highly disappointing". Fine. Thing is, they're almost all guaranteed to be watchable overall. Unwatchable means that it is *unwatchable*. Bad enough that it's damn near impossible to give it your full attention for an hour-and-a-half. Unwatchable is when a movie is so boring you wish you could sleep, yet so annoyed that you stay up with a headache. You cringe and cry yourself into a coma of boredom. The plot is non-existent. The director is out-to-lunch. The acting makes your eyes glaze over. Yet somehow, (usually due to a demand for financial re-coup) the production company decided to not only finish the film but release it to the public. When it comes to entertainment, these are the bottom of the barrel. They aren't fun-bad, they're just plain bad. They're the worst of the worst! They should be completely avoided by anyone not fully trained in the previous four categories mentioned.

It's worth noting that we're excluding non-fiction, documentaries, and propaganda films. There exist many political, religious, and conspiratorial "films" out there which are heavily rallied against, laughed at and collected. Yes, many of those are sought after and jokingly mocked within collecting circles. Heck, there's an entire subgenre of 1970s and 1980s fear-based propaganda films which have been aptly dubbed "fear-porn". The problem is, they drift quite far from what most people would traditionally refer to as a "*movie*", and therefore are not included in this book. They cross the lines from entertainment to propaganda. Unless you're already super familiar with bad cinema in general, it's not recommended. That's a stage to graduate to, should one grow bored of collecting conventional crap. Too often those films are written and directed with genuine malice towards specific groups of people. By "movies" we're talking about fictitious entertainment and not real-life prejudices that exploit the medium of film.

Anyway, now that we've established some of the different categories of "bad", it's probably a good idea to specifically list some of those notorious films you should familiarize yourself with. Relax! Assuming you have a sense of humor, these are all watchable. About 2/3rds of these films have original VHS releases. If you want to understand the full scope of things, it's worth including more recent and modern-day trash cinema too. Bad films are not contained in any one specific era.

The following movies fall along the lines of the first two categories — campy, silly and ridiculous. Films so cheesy and inept they make you giggle just as much as cringe.

1. *The Room* (2003)
2. *Plan 9 From Outer Space* (1959)
3. *Troll 2* (1990)
4. *Tales from the QuadeaD Zone* (1987)
5. *Manos: The Hands of Fate* (1966)
6. *Birdemic: Shock and Terror* (2010)
7. *Fateful Findings* (2013)
8. *Alien Private Eye* (1989)
9. *Frankenstein Island* (1981)
10. *The Garbage Pail Kids Movie* (1987)

The first three films listed above are not only some of the most celebrated bad flicks, they even have films/documentaries based on just how bad they are. That's right - they were so infamous that other directors had to document their level of atrociousness. Their praise goes well beyond a traditional cult-following and has attained worldwide recognition in their sheer incompetence!

Watch the remainder of that list and you'll wonder how the scripts even got greenlit to begin with. They're hilarious in their dialogue, laughable in their directing. They span the gamut from high budget to low, from Hollywood to backyard productions. It's safe to say that one of the reasons they are so great is that they *try*. They didn't go for bad-on-purpose. It happened by accident. Perhaps you might argue that *The Garbage Pail Kids* (1987) knew that it would be somewhat terrible given its base concept. However, with a budget of $1,000,000 USD, it's hard to justify the raging inferno of cringe that all that money produced.

These are the top choices when it comes to introducing someone to bad cinema. If you haven't seen any of them, it's worth watching at least one or two in order to have a full understanding of filmmaking in general. Why? I mean, you've probably watched great films already, right? Who hasn't browsed through some list of the Top 100 Films Ever Made and noted that you've already seen a bunch? Most people are familiar with excellent films. The problem is that if you don't understand the follies of filmmaking, you only know half the story. How much of the younger generation is growing up with automated recommendations via Netflix algorithms? Heck, how many adults ever bother to watch a bad flick on purpose? Back in the video store days, it happened far more often. Through those experiences, we began to (perhaps unconsciously) understand how difficult it is to make a blockbuster hit. Sometimes, a film went sideways. It just happened. Maybe the director had a drinking problem. Maybe the editor didn't get paid and butchered the film last minute. Or maybe it was just incompetent casting coupled with an inexperienced crew. Bad movies happened more than we'd like to think. A well-rounded film buff knows to be sympathetic to that. It puts moviemaking into perspective and helps you understand the difficulties a film production can face.

As mentioned, not all "bad" films are unintentional. Sometimes writers and directors set out to purposely make a so-bad-it's-good movie, simply to get a smirk (and sneer) out of people. Their goal is notoriety. There exist hundreds of these shlockbusters, all trying to out-cringe one another. The following three flicks are staples of bad-on-purpose cinema:

1. *The Toxic Avenger* (1984)
2. *Attack of the Killer Tomatoes* (1988)
3. *Sharknado* (2013)

The first two listed were so influential and infamous that they spawned sequels, cartoons, action figures, and even stage plays. They're two of the most flagrant bad-on-purpose flicks to ever grace VHS. They've transcended bad cinema and permeated the broader spectrum of entertainment. The third, *Sharknado* (2013), is a more recent installment in this category. It has garnished such rabid infamy within film culture that it deserves to be in third place and seems to be spawning endless made-for-tv sequels. Their directors all keep comedy at the forefront, coupled with over-the-top performances in full view. They utilize dark, low-brow gallows humor to propel them into complete and utter notoriety.

Okay, we need to mention some examples of "The Unwatchable". If you really want to watch some steaming piles of tired and boring crap, feast your eyes on these. They're overly long, poorly edited, unfunny, grinding snooze-fests. The kind of films you storm out of the theatre 1/3rd of the way in. The kind of movie rental that you would return to the local video store and not only complain but demand a refund *and* an apology. Be thankful we are only listing three:

1. *Nukie* (1987)
2. *Night of Horror* (1981)
3. *Moment by Moment* (1978)

These aren't funny-bad. They're boring bad. Fall asleep bad. They're stellar examples of stale acting, tedious writing, and awful directing. Twenty minutes in and I guarantee you look at your watch, cringe, then wonder if it still counts as having "watched" it if you fast-forward to the end. No, that doesn't count. Look, just don't watch them at all! Instead, watch online film bloggers mock them. Life is too short. Plus, it's the only way you'll get any sort of pleasure from them. At least they have that *one* redeeming value: *mockery*. They're super fun to trash-talk!

Finally, take into consideration what many producers and directors have argued within the context of "bad" cinema: that the worst, *truly* worst films of all, are simply the ones you forgot about an hour after watching. The unremarkable movies you can't even remember seeing. The mediocre Hollywood hit that didn't illicit *any* emotional response from you. It left no imprint. It taught you nothing. Pure fluff instantly dispatched to the back of your mind, never again to see the light of day. You can't hate it; you don't even remember watching it to begin with. Now that's just sad.

A typical busy Blockbuster night in 1990.

A gutted and empty Blockbuster in 2020.

"Quick Drop" drop box for after-hours VHS returns.

A long-lost Video Vendor machine (Photo by Jerry Kohnen).

The epic VHS collection of Michael Votto.

Will Foran's gigantic wall of tapes.

Scene from a Blockbuster employee training video.

A 90s Blockbuster commercial advertisement.

Dougglass Antonio Alcala III lost in tapes.

A small piece of Maurice Kenny's replica video store collection.

Wizard Video care of collector Daniel Chockley.

Ultra-rare Canadian Vogue Video.

Maurice Kenny — demonstrating the fine art of rack display.

The extensive VHS room of Zach Murphree.

Tape galore care of Chuck Bronson.

Tapes, tapes and more tapes care of Danny Wilkez.

The VHS horde of Freddy Nuckels.

The personal collection of Joe Climan.

8. Rise of The Rip-offs

Okay, we've covered ground on some of the more desirable tapes, from shlock horror to bad cinema. There's something for every VHS collector out there. SOV tapes are always great due to their minuscule budgets and often rushed output. Terrible B-movies are a staple too. Horror is typically the genre of choice among tapeheads. Are there any other categories or styles of film worth mentioning in the greater context of tape collecting? Well, yes! We can break things down just a wee bit further and explore not only the exploitation of the home video boom but of specific film titles themselves. Where money is flowing, expect exploitation at its finest. As you might guess, there are multiple avenues of exploitation throughout cinema as a whole. For every smash Hollywood hit, there was a production company out there thinking, "How can we ride this wave?" For every horror classic, there was a director in Italy or Spain trying to rip it off. For every cheesy film that somehow surpassed expectations, there was a person at a typewriter scripting endless sequels. It was a gravy train that everyone wanted to hop on...and hop on they did.

Back in the 1970s, hit horror films like *Jaws* (1975), *The Exorcist* (1973), *Dawn of the Dead* (1978), *Alien* (1979) and *Halloween* (1978) were cleaning up and making quite an impact in their theatrical runs. People were having visceral reactions throughout film-houses and local drive-ins were raking in customers. Not only that, but overseas audiences were appreciating those American hits all the same. Adventure and sci-fi films like *Star Wars* (1977) and *Planet of the Apes* (1974) were absolute cash cows, raking in millions of dollars worldwide at the box office. Eventually, foreign producers would note that there was a market emerging far greater than anyone had predicted. Sure, the motion picture industry had been a staple in the world of entertainment for decades; however, only now was it *really* starting to look lucrative. Some lucky producers became multi-millionaires overnight. Actors became household names. Hit directors were revered as artistic geniuses. Everyone wanted a piece of the pie, and Hollywood wasn't the only place you could make a movie.

Terms like "knock-offs" and "rip-offs" are almost too broad, encompassing a few different varieties of exploitation. Let's really refine the categories down for further for clarity.

Mockbusters: Low-budget movies that purposely mimic and copy a specific film in order to capitalize on the hype or concept behind the original. They'll steal the initial idea, give it a similar name or title, and sometimes even release it a week or two before the official film! They might take aim at audiences who are unaware of the existence of the original film, other times targeting oblivious folks who simply don't know the difference between the original and the mockbuster. They exist to capitalize on a trend or flavor within any given moment of filmmaking, throwing all taste out the window to the point of being considered a clone.

Illegitimate Sequels: Popular throughout Europe and South America in the 1970s and 80s, illegitimate sequels are self-explanatory — Movies commissioned to act as fake sequels to popular Hollywood hits. Sometimes, they even stole the original film's title and stuck a "Part 2" on the cover. They operated semi-legally, occasionally getting into trouble with lawsuits. To play it safe, by the time they made it to the American market, the film would have been renamed to something completely different and given brand new artwork. Truly, filmmaking at its most devious.

Parodies: Movies that parody and poke fun at more popular films. They take the original film's premise and plot, then basically turn it into a comedy version. Usually parody films rely on slapstick humor, but they can blur the lines between a mockbuster and a comedic interpretation depending on how they are marketed to the public. Funny enough, this gimmick has been exploited to its highest degree within the world of adult films and XXX cinema.

Exploitation Films: Niche B-movies that financially exploit a specific trend or subgenre of film. Blaxploitation, cannibal films, slashers, splatter films, sexploitation and mondo films are just a few examples of how specific subgenres can be milked to produce countless cheap movies. If there's a fanbase, there's a film being made for it, even if it is low budget trash. It's also popular for a hit film to be exploited to produce many cheap sequels. Although they might be officially licensed spin-offs, those sequels are often pumped out in a manner that one could describe as lacking in good taste. They end up more like a product or commodity rather than art.

While this all sounds terribly money-driven, and it is, none of it would exist if there wasn't a demand for it. Sure, many folks simply enjoy trashy and weird films. However, people went to the cinema or rented a VHS to see something *unique*, even if it wasn't a well-rated blockbuster hit. If it promised something extreme (be it nudity, violence or bad humor), there was an interest.

Although money and profit were the driving factor, many of those rip-off flicks coming out of Europe gained cult-fandom status. Back in the early 1980s, it was commonplace for writers and directors in places like Italy to approach production companies with an original idea, only to receive the question, "So which American film is this based on?" That should tell you everything about the climate of film production in that part of the world. If you were an investor, you could hedge your bet and almost guarantee financial recoup if it was an exploitation of an American hit. Obviously, that was a problem as that premise lacks any artistic merit. However, most of those directors didn't lack any artistry themselves; instead they pushed the limits of their confines, doing their best to implement original ideas and concepts into mockbusters and illegitimate foreign sequels.

Throughout the 1950s, monster flicks such as *The Monster of Piedras Blanca* (1959) would take more than a hint of inspiration from the more popular *Creature From The Black Lagoon* (1954). The Filipino film *Batman Fights Dracula* (1967) defied any trademark or copyright regulation. The movie *Angels Revenge* (1979) had more than a passing resemblance to the 1970s *Charlie's Angels* television show. These are just a few early examples. Throughout Mexico, Europe, and the Middle East, straight-up knockoff flicks would propagate without much legal trouble. Horror hits like *Dawn of the Dead* (1978) would receive illegitimate sequels like *Zombi 2* (1979). Although financial gain through exploiting the original film was the primary goal, it was around this time that US audiences took notice of directors like Lucio Fulci (who directed *Zombi 2*, more simply known as "Zombie"). Although it was exploitation-based, the cinematography and directing was far more unique than the average low-budget zombie knock-off. Directors like Fulci brought to the table a psychedelic style which paired well alongside fellow giallo filmmakers like Dario Argento — known best for his supernatural epic, *Susperia* (1977). There was a palpable atmosphere of off-kilter suspense (and, perhaps, drug-inspired cinematography) that was genuinely unique to their films. Fulci and fellow Italian exploitation filmmakers began to catch the attention of film fans across America. US-based distributors, like the previously mentioned Wizard Video, were more than happy to bring them to video stores and VCRs across North America. Some were terrifying glimpses into the world of foreign fright-flicks. Others, such as *Hell of The Living Dead* (1980) and *Nightmare City* (1980) relied on ubiquitous blood, gore, and nudity to hold their viewers' attention.

Unsurprisingly, this scheme worked fantastically on young boys throughout the USA. Fans began to take note of how certain directors, despite being hired guns for foreign exploitation, had legitimate directing chops and genuine artistic vision.

Continuing into the 1980s, things would only ramp up as home video took hold. Some Hollywood films like *Mac and Me* (1988) were homegrown American cash-ins, barely even hiding the fact that it was a rip-off of *E.T. the Extra-terrestrial* (1982). Hits like *Friday the 13th* (1980) spawned not only a franchise but an entire genre of "slasher" films, all hoping to achieve sleeper-hit status. Although the subgenre of slasher films already existed, *Friday the 13th* significantly ramped it up to inspire innumerable clones.

Although one can say the horror genre is perhaps the best (or most notorious) illustration of exploitation, don't think that the action genre didn't have its fair share of knockoffs. Heroic characters such as Batman, Spiderman, Superman, and even James Bond were given countless unlicensed overseas renditions. Turkey, Brazil, and Mexico were well known for putting out their own unofficial versions throughout the 1970s and 80s. Sometimes they even mixed franchises! If you can think of a popular action film from that time period, expect a foreign knockoff to have been made. While the comedy genre wasn't as ripe with rip-offs back then, there were certainly questionable "sequels" — that is, completely original films which American companies tried to pass off as a sequel to a popular comedy franchise. Look no further than the cheesy *Meatballs* series for an example of exploiting a pre-existing brand and fanbase.

One of the more prophetic mockbusters of the 1990's was *Carnosaur* (1993) - a killer-dinosaur flick released two weeks before the much-hyped Hollywood blockbuster, *Jurassic Park* (1993). Although it wasn't directly scripted to be a *Jurassic Park* clone, the marketing and release was quite the coincidence. Soon after, *Dinosaurs from the Deep* (1993) and *Dinosaur Island* (1994) came out, utilizing the same concept. Where the eyes go, money follows, and the 1990s just loved dinosaurs.

You might say *Carnosaur* was, in a sense, "prophetic" in that it was a full decade before the more blatant and obvious era of mockbusters were ushered in. Once the 2000s hit, production companies like Asylum Films began unabashedly pumping out *unquestionable* mockbusters straight-to-video. Movies like *Transmorphers* (2007) were obvious clones of bigger hits like *Transformers* (2007). However, this was so utterly blatant and in-your-face that instead of taking offense, moviegoers would pick up the DVD case, laugh and then rent it. Audiences were now in on the joke. Producing dozens of films with similar storylines, cover art, and even near-identical film titles, Asylum Films show no sign of stopping. They blur the lines between parody, mockbuster, and illegitimate sequels, preferring the phrase "*tie-in*". That's right. Apparently, films like *Titanic II* (2010) are — ahem! — tie-ins. Sure, why not?

Direct-to-DVD production companies like Asylum Films certainly took leads from the previous direct-to-VHS model, capitalizing on home video sales. Of course, today, DVD sales are low, with those companies relying more on streaming services, online and network television. There will always be a market for low-budget exploitation films. As mentioned in the previous chapter, 1980s shot-on-video VHS are almost all collectible in some way, partly due to the scarcity, partly due to the low quality. Many fans have been growing more and more rabid in their SOV and direct-to-tape acquisitions.

While most VHS collectors don't specifically target mockbusters or illegitimate sequels, you can be sure to spot dozens in almost any collection. They were so plentiful throughout the golden age of tape that it's almost impossible to work your way around exploitation films. Some collectors do enjoy hunting down foreign knock-off versions, along with imported rip-offs from South America. Many of those films have gone viral on the internet due to their ridiculous attempt to cash in on superior big-budget flicks. That's right, we're circling right back to the realm of bad movies all over again — this time, overseas! It's no surprise that they were quite inept and cut corners all over the place. Bad acting, atrocious directing, and raw editing coupled with the fact that they were also trying to clone bigger and more popular films — it's both depressing and hilarious.

Again, it's important to understand that all those filmmakers were working under serious duress: Ultra-low budgets, scornful investors, and Hollywood-hungry audiences. All obstacles they needed to navigate. From the depth of exploitation emerged some hidden-gem directors and classic B-movies that VHS collectors and cinephiles have built entire fanbases around — not due to their hokey appeal, but to an appreciation of artistry under constraint.

9. Think Outside the Box

One concept worth digging a little deeper into is the notion of inventiveness through limitation — In other words, pushing the boundaries of a platform out of *necessity*. In the case of present-day multimedia, there's a lot less of that happening. What can be said about the boundaries of VHS and the distribution and consumption of home video? Well, to say that it had its restrictions would be an understatement. Whether you were a privately-owned video store, a distribution company or an advertiser, you had to use creativity. Fortunately, the 80s and 90s had that in spades!

We've already established that giant big boxes and raunchy cover art were a mainstay within the realm of home video. A film was relegated to a small piece of shelf space where it had to fight for eyeballs. What was considered too much? What was considered too little? These were questions that both distributors and store owners would mull over daily. Although it might seem like a mere afterthought, keep in mind this is how many folks made a living. Home video paid some peoples mortgages and put food on the table. So how did they fight to stand out in a crowd and stay relevant?

Around 1990, a few distribution companies started to design specialized cases with embossed artwork and lenticular hologram-like covers. Movies like *Demon Wind* (1990) featured a VHS release with a lenticular cover which made it look like the titular demon monster was smashing through a window as you wiggled the box side-to-side. *Frankenhooker* (1990) had a button and a speaker on the front; when you pressed the button, the case would cry out, "Wanna date?" *Dead Pit* (1989) and *Metamorphosis* (1990) both featured characters on their cover art with light-up LED eyes. *Mirror, Mirror* (1990) utilized a good old-fashioned hologram of the villain on the cover, specifically embedded into the mirror drawn in the cover art. These companies strove for new and innovative ways to make physical VHS releases more interesting. This continued into the late 1990s with gimmicky VHS boxes for films like *Bleeders* (1997), *Jack Frost* (1997), and *The Night Flier* (1997).

If the VHS box art and synopsis were all you could go by, were there any instances of complete exaggeration? Yes. As mentioned earlier, distributors like Genesis Home Video would often acquire rights to a film where they would create such drastically different artwork that it barely resembled the film at all. Their release of *Revenge of the Zombie* (1988) was, in fact, *Kiss Daddy Goodbye* (1981), simply repackaged with an alternate title card, artwork, and date. They used a 1980s stage prop (from Nightmares FX via Starlog Press) in a photo shoot to create the cover art — virtually unrelated to anything in the film. Does it look impressive? Definitely! But this was merely a trick to sell a previously released flick as something new. Various companies would try and pass off older films with new packaging and artwork. Whether ethical or not, it was an effective ruse for many VHS distribution companies throughout the 1980s.

By now you shouldn't be surprised that it was mainly horror films given special VHS box art treatment. Perhaps this goes even deeper than the simple "lost genre" principal behind horror flicks being so sought after? Even back in the day, horror films *themselves* referenced home video and VHS. *Videodrome* (1983) featured several VHS references, including a lead character whose torso literally mutates and transforms into a VCR. *Remote Control* (1988) was about video store clerks who discover an alien plot to take over the earth via VHS tapes that brainwash and control their viewers. *Video Violence* (1987) deals with a newly opened video store receiving a snuff-like murder tape, only to discover the town's dark obsession with "video violence". The cover art itself features a videotape and VCR. Even in the early millennium, *The Ring* (2002) was essentially about a cursed videotape which kills its victims seven days after viewing.

Beyond the movies and their box art, video stores themselves had to fight for attention. There was always a threat of looming competition, and therefore you needed something to make you stand out. Perhaps *standees,* giant cardboard cut-outs of actors, robots and monsters? Why not? In the early days, most video stores looked like libraries. By the mid-90s, they looked more like film sets. Standees of action heroes, extra-large posters, gumball machines, mannequins, strange pop-up advertisements, and other bizarre physical media littered the shop floor. Some horror sections looked more like walk-through haunted houses and Halloween shops! Popcorn machines and huge shelves of candy were often present. Video stores would often try and one-up each other, all the while trying to find a balance between entertainment and professionalism.

By the late 1980s/early 1990s, some film producers decided to try another creative tactic to sell tapes: infomercials and TV ads. Probably the most notorious of all sold-on-television VHS was the *Dorf* series: Half-hour comedy sketches featuring Tim Conway (on his knees) as the four-foot-tall Dorf character, attempting to make some sort of pseudo-instructional video for the viewer. The tapes were sold for $29.99 + shipping. Manufactured out of Los Angeles, they were equally ridiculous as they were politically incorrect. One of the back-cover taglines to *Dorf On Golf* (1987) should tell you everything, simply stating "These folks give new meaning to the word 'handicap'." Yep. Not exactly high comedy. Regardless, a certain amount of folks shelled out their hard-earned cash for them.

A good analogy to help illustrate this chapter would be that of an artistic platform such as music. Many songwriters will tell you that in order to push the boundaries of a composition, you need to have those proverbial walls to push against. With music (especially electronic music in the year 2020), it helps to limit yourself to a small and specific set of *instruments* which you can then experiment with. Having no narrow options where "the sky is the limit" often yields too many choices and not enough restrictions. The comparison to 1980s and 90s home video is that only when you have such a limited platform to work with can you truly exhaust and test the barriers of creativity. Because it was so limited, the business of home video slowly became one of creative and artistic flourishing. Sometimes for better, sometimes for worse! When thinking outside the box becomes necessary for survival, it becomes a culture where creativity is not only reinforced but heightened.

This certainly doesn't mean that modern-day films and digital streaming services are without creative merit. Netflix shows like *Black Mirror*'s "Bandersnatch" episode is presented as an interactive film, where the viewer is given an option to choose which direction the plot and character go in. With a dozen different possible endings, this choose-your-own-adventure style of filmmaking is a radical new approach to the world of film. Movies like *Hardcore Henry* (2016) utilize present-day GoPro cameras to create a "first-person" style of filmography where you experience the film through the eyes of the lead character. Advancements in 3D technology have allowed films like *Avatar* (2009) to dazzle the eyes far beyond the mediocre blue-and-red 3D gimmick of the 1980s.

Sure, some folks might look back on 80s/90s home video as gimmicky, but many respectable ideas and creative outputs were produced throughout those decades. Film itself went through an evolution — both in its production and consumption. Marketing departments, graphic designers, filmmakers, and entrepreneurs were all put to the test — forced to exhaust all artistic merit and experiment endlessly. It was a time of breaking new ground. While nostalgia alone is relatively pointless, celebration and enjoyment of that time period can be healthy. Having a developed understanding of our entertainment industry helps us fully recognize the good and bad aspects of it, and perhaps more importantly, how to move forward.

10. Oh, The Horror!

There's a moment in many a VHS collector's life when they're called out for collecting horror and exploitation flicks. There are claims that cinema throughout the 1970s, 80s, and 90s was exploitation at its worst — ripe with misogyny and violence. Very little redeeming about those films, right? We've heard about how the collectors of said tapes are supporting a genre where females were cast as nothing but victims of toxic patriarchy. Nothing but garbage for gore-hounds that promote violence against women and are celebrating a bygone era of a problematic society. This chapter will analyze whether these accusations stand true or are exaggerations which conveniently omit valid counterpoints.

First of all, there were literally *thousands* of horror films produced and distributed on VHS in North America during that timeframe. It would take years to analyze even a small fraction of them on an individual basis. The best we can do is to take the most widely distributed series, subgenres, and distribution companies, then work downwards into less prevalent films, all the while attempting to give honest examinations of key titles and entries throughout.

If we're going to start anywhere, we should begin with the three most well-known franchises within horror: *A Nightmare on Elm Street* (1984), *Friday the 13th* (1980), and *Halloween* (1978). To the uninitiated, that would be the popular villains Freddy Krueger, Jason Voorhees, and Michael Myers. They are by far the most famous and widely distributed horror series. They have dozens of sequels and remakes. They've spawned spin-off comics and video games. They've been parodied in kids cartoons and every Halloween store in North America sells their costumes. They've become not only horror classics but *genre icons*. However, all three also feature women being stalked and murdered by monstrous killers. But is it fair to summarize them like that?

Not if you consider the fact that men are also killed or placed in peril. We're not going to make a death-count for each individual film, but even casual viewing will demonstrate that the ratio of men vs. women being threated or killed is very close to *equal*. What about the fact that the killers are male? You may want to consider the fact that in many of these films, the killer isn't human but instead either a zombified Frankenstein-like monster or a multi-dimensional shapeshifting boogeyman. That doesn't completely change the fact, it's just worth pointing out. Many of the villains aren't considered human. Even then, do the antagonists identifying as male signify misogyny? Even when he or "it" is attacking men in an equal fashion? You can't ignore the fact that in all three of these series, the protagonists are almost always female. In other words, you have a female lead, who is the hero, killing or at least stopping a male antagonist. In most of these series, the villain meets a bloody and violent end. Those protagonists are often portrayed as normal everyday women. When placed into a life or death situation, they end up evolving into brave and heroic archetypes. Can you say the same thing about action films of the 1970s, 80s, and 90s? Don't answer. We'll be coming back to that. It's an important point, but let's explore some additional series and see if they differ.

The next three most popular franchises would be *Hellraiser* (1987), *The Texas Chainsaw Massacre* (1974), and *Child's Play* (1988). For those unfamiliar, you might know them by their infamous bad guys: Pinhead, Leatherface, and Chucky. All three series are so well known within the genre that they're still birthing sequels today. They have their own dolls, toys and comic books. So, what do we find when we analyze them? We find the exact same scenario: male antagonists (often semi-human) chasing and murdering both women and men in close to equal numbers. In all three series, the villains are either stopped, or utterly defeated, by women. If they're not defeated, then the lead heroine escapes and leaves the killer badly injured. Is it misogynistic if the victims are both male and female? Or, if we see women taking on and adopting heroic roles? Now we need to be fair and say that other women are at times seen topless or half-nude on screen. However, this is only in two of the six series mentioned, which isn't completely out of place considering the frequency of nudity within any Rated-R films of any genre. It's also worth noting that it's typically not the lead actress, and is often a rather brief scene. We shouldn't just gloss over nudity, but occasional female nudity on screen alone doesn't exactly constitute misogyny. Especially if the context is that of a summer camp, where a mixed group of men and women all strip down to go swimming. Or a young couple, both topless and in the bedroom. Sleazy? Yep. But there is a difference between brief nudity and full-out female exploitation.

Let's look beyond the popular franchises and focus on some individual fan favorites. Every top 10 horror list will almost always contain at least two, if not all three, of the following genre films: *Dawn of the Dead* (1978), *The Exorcist* (1973), and *Susperia* (1977). You're bound to have at least heard of these, even if you don't know much about scary movies. *Dawn of the Dead*, a film where we find the lead female character fleeing a zombie apocalypse with three male cohorts — where it's mostly men attacked and killed by zombies — a film where the female lead survives unscathed, unlike two of the three male leads. How about *The Exorcist*? Here we find the roles reversed: we have a female antagonist (once again, not really "human") who survives, and the lead male protagonist is killed. How about *Susperia*? I mean, women are murdered a lot in that film, right? Yes, by other women. In fact, the film takes place in a ballet school with mostly women, yet that doesn't stop men from being murdered on screen as well. Again, it features female villains where it's debatable to even call the antagonists human; they're supernatural witches with inhuman powers.

Let's try some of the most well-known *monster* films: *The Thing* (1982), *The Fly* (1986), and *The Blob* (1988). Obviously monster movies, just judging by their titles alone! In fact, all three are successful remakes of older monster movies. *The Thing*, where a male protagonist and a dozen other men (and only men) are killed on-screen by a shape-shifting alien. *The Fly*, where a man is accidentally transformed into a mutant insect and, after maiming a few other men, attempts to abduct the female lead who finally kills him. *The Blob*, a movie about a giant voracious (and genderless) blob that rolls around eating and devouring men and women indiscriminately. Other notable monster films include *Critters* (1986), *CHUD* (1984), and *Gremlins* (1984). All three of those were popular enough to spawn sequels (for better or worse) and all three feature a pretty safe ratio of men and women in peril from various non-human monsters.

Keep in mind, we're still focused on analyzing notable well-known and well-distributed films within the genre. Does that demonstrate the vast majority of horror films being without misogyny? No. Again, there are literally thousands of films to go through. At this point, let's get to the crux of the argument. The following are two simple points which often confuse the casual moviegoer and force them to choose one side or another, which is a mistake:

#1. There are titles within horror/exploitation that are totally and unmistakably misogynist. These are what we will call the "*worst offenders*".

#2. There are titles within horror/exploitation that feature some of the most powerful female roles in cinematic history. These are what we'll call "*positive examples*".

Now, the argument of this book is basically that the latter is more prevalent, and here's why:

Let's take a glance at two of the worst offenders: *Guinea Pig: Flower of Flesh and Blood* (1985), and *The New York Ripper* (1982). These are films in which women are not only killed but done so in slow and in excruciatingly bloody detail. Not much is given to the female roles in these films; they are merely dolls to be ravaged. Few men in them experience the same fate. Not much more to say than that — these films are terrible when it comes to the treatment of women.

* FYI: this book is outright excluding hyper-violent "softcore" independent SOV releases from the conversation. In other words, no-budget adult-oriented violent exploitation that borders on pornographic material. Again, we're focusing on fictitious films, not XXX entertainment. Some movies may blur that line, but for practical reasons, we must draw a wide line here. Please don't write in saying, "You're ignoring flicks like Porno Slaughter Orgy Pt. 17*!". For all intents and purposes, that's not what this book considers a horror movie. **

Two counterpoint positive examples would be films like *Alien* (1979) and *Silence of the Lambs* (1991), both horror films heralded for containing two of the toughest and most genuinely fierce heroines in film history. And yes, Alien was horror. Sci-fi horror, but the series tagline "*In space, no one can hear you scream*" should tell you exactly which genre it was rooted in. Series such as *Alien* (and even flicks like *Halloween*) not only feature women in strong protagonist roles but continue this trend even in their respective sequels — often with the same actress reprising the same character. Many consider these roles to be icons of feminism as they display women taking control of their own fate, unlike just about every other genre of that period where women in peril are set up to be saved by men.

Now, consider that between these two extremes is a place where most horror films lie. A huge grey area.

When discussing these two polarizing areas, why should one category carry more weight? Well, a fair thing to consider is their development and distribution. The positive examples you'll find are all films that bombarded theaters and large-scale cinemas. They featured big budgets and were widely distributed all over the home video market. They were so prevalent that it would be absurd to find a video store missing these titles. They were frequently shown, heavily pushed, widely distributed and commercially available films. Can we say the same about the worst offenders? Not at all. Those were rare, obscure grindhouse flicks at best. Many of the most misogynistic titles were so scarce that they were only released limited direct-to-video. Some were shot-on-video and distributed with companies that disappeared quickly after. Many of those tapes go for hundreds of dollars on eBay, merely due to how exceptionally rare they are. Most horror films within the "worst offenders" category are so obscure that it could take you years to track down original copies.

      You might make a chicken-and-egg argument that the worst offenders were merely forced into grindhouse drive-ins and that the positive examples were lifted to Hollywood stardom due to how great they were. But that's not typically how film production and distribution works. Yes, a great film *can* occasionally rise and be pushed by a solid fanbase, but usually those flicks are propped up from day one. They're given a decent budget and solid theatrical push. *Rarely* does a film go from no-budget to national, politically correct or not.

      When weighing these two polarizing sides, we need to consider their production, development, and distribution. You can't paint a genre with such a large brush when all things are not even close to being equal (as far as viewing and prevalence goes). Again, it's important to consider that this whole dichotomy completely ignores the fact that there's a huge body of horror films which take a balanced and fair ratio of male-to-female characters, protagonists and villains. Fans of the genre who've been exposed to many of its films will echo this sentiment: Yes, there are misogynistic films, and yes there are films showing powerful female roles. However, the latter is more common, especially for what could be found at any given moment on a random store shelf in the 1980s and 90s.

We also don't need to make any role-reversal analogies, because that already exists. There is a plethora of horror films where the killer is female. Giallo horror films became a *cliché* subgenre for featuring women antagonists.

There is a good point to be made regarding "moments of peril" — specifically, the camera time that displays women in destress vs. men. Studies have shown that most horror movies, on average, will show a woman in stress and peril up to 3x – 4x longer than their male counterparts *(Linz, Daniel; Donnerstein, Edward, 1994. "Dialogue: Sex and Violence in Slasher Films: A Reinterpretation". Journal of Broadcasting & Electronic Media)*. This is a fair and perhaps obvious criticism and a fact that can't be ignored. The directors utilize the female archetype and exploit the damsel-in-distress scenario to no end. While this doesn't equate malice, it's a point in the argument against horror (albeit an obvious one). An armed male character in distress simply won't coerce the same emotional reaction on screen. It seems to be more along the lines of writers and directors being lazy and making cheap thrills produced with cut-rate scare tactics. Sleazy and cheap, sure, but not evidence of calculated hate and prejudice.

Nothing exists in a vacuum, so here is a final point: other genres, specifically the 1970s and 80s action and comedy films, were equally as bad, if not worse. Think of a bunch of popular action and comedy flicks from that time, then try and list the great female protagonists of those genres. Sarah Connor from *Terminator 2* perhaps? Yup. A classic action heroine. Other than her, there's not a lot. Now try and list the number of those films with gratuitous female nudity, inappropriate jokes, harassment, sexual assault, or movies where women are reduced to arm candy and child-like damsels-in-distress. You'll discover far more in those latter categories.

Go back and re-watch some classic 80s comedies like *Loose Screws* (1985), *Porky's* (1981) or *Meatballs 3* (1986). Those popular, mainstream and classic Hollywood flicks were simply oozing with misogyny. Watch them with your daughter and be forced to explain why the "heroes" are one step away from being frat-boy rapists. If those were horror films, those lead characters would be killed off in the first half-hour.

Is collecting problematic films problematic in itself? That all depends on the motive for collecting in the first place. The mere act of archiving isn't equal to "celebrating" a specific film. It's merely showcasing a lost format of our culture within a specific window of time, warts and all. Unless a movie is seriously vile or propagandistic (and most films put out on major VHS labels were certainly not), most collectors have no problem acknowledging that a particular film is standing on poor moral ground. It's archived as a reflection of its time. From the very beginnings of cinema, we have evolved our line of thinking and the way we implement equality and morality throughout society. "To the moon, Alice!" was the phrase coined by Jackie Gleason's character Ralph on the hit 1950s TV show *The Honeymooners*. This was in reference to him threatening to punch her — a threat of all-too-common domestic violence within 1950s America. Obviously, this would not be tolerated today. Those problematic TV shows are not denied; they are acknowledged as what they were: mostly funny, but also of-their-time and featuring some very problematic writing. We already mentioned the overtly racist portrayal of an Asian man in *Breakfast at Tiffanies*. The film won multiple awards and was a smash Hollywood hit. Looking back, we can acknowledge the technical and artistic merits while *also* acknowledging the yellow-face character as being insulting and degrading. There are many examples of problematic characters and plotlines within 1950s – 1990s cinema, not just in the genre of horror.

Compartmentalization of enjoyment vs. admission of immorality within a film can be an issue, but part of the solution is to fully admit when something has elements of misogyny, racism, homophobia, or prejudice. It doesn't mean that owning a specific tape is unwarranted; just be ready to admit how and where a specific movie has less-than-desirable qualities.

The idea of "throwing out the baby with the bathwater" can be a dangerous one as well. Probably the best example of this is the classic horror film *Night of The Living Dead* (1968). It was initially slammed as nothing but gory terror, with Variety even labeling it as an "unrelieved orgy of sadism." In retrospect, the violence in that film isn't too shocking in the year 2020. However, it's more than worth noting that it's regarded as the first film — not just a horror film, but the first film *period* — to depict a lead black male without referencing his race. In other words, actor Duane Jones was given the lead role not because he was black but simply because, as director George Romero put it, "He simply gave the best audition." The role was written for anyone; it just so happens that the person who got it was black. While that might be common today, it was a huge deal back in 1968. Sadly, that was unheard of back then.

That kind of casting call helped usher in a new line of thinking when it came to breaking down racial barriers within the world of film. Similar kudos should go to *Alien* (1979) for having an epic and heroic female lead while the rest of the cast is killed off. No white knight swooping in to save the damsel in distress in her final moments. Many subversive horror titles are in the unique position of being able to experiment and attack social norms — many of which need to be broken down.

We should acknowledge and admit when a specific film is problematic vs. simply poor in quality. We should recognize and defend when a movie breaks down social norms and pushes us to better understand basic concepts of equality. We should keep in mind that films progress alongside a society; for better or for worse, they are a reflection of their time. We should understand those entire genres cannot be painted with such a wide brush. They mirror both the good and bad aspects of where we come from. They all have elements to celebrate and elements to criticize. Some so more than others, yes, but if we can celebrate the empowering aspects while exposing and criticizing the negatives, only then can we shine a light on the full spectrum of cinema and its reflection of morality.

11. The Video Dead

When it comes to collecting films on a physical medium, it's evident that VHS has a surging demand, along with DVD. In fact, you'd probably assume DVD is the winner as far as collecting goes. Many department stores still sell them by the hundreds. They're still in mass production, along with Blu-ray, and especially prevalent throughout thrift stores and pawn shops. Sure, people are *buying* them, but are they *collecting* them in the same way people collect other formats? Are they *hunting* for them, or just casually purchasing movies to watch at their leisure? That's where things begin to differ. Perhaps the question can be phrased like this: Do people romanticize DVD and Blu-ray the same way they romanticize VHS?

It's a good idea to explore other collectible commercial film formats in order to understand why said formats *do* or *do not* elicit the same fervor as VHS. Some of these formats are modern, others we'll call "the video dead": forgotten film platforms which never really caught on. They were immediately dead in the water. We'll start off with the highest-quality format, then work our way down to the bottom:

Blu-ray

The highest quality of any physical medium of home video. Even better than DVD and in many ways its successor. Blu-ray began development circa 2001 and began commercial releases in 2006. It has the same physical appearance as a CD, only with 25 GB per layer, with dual-layer discs at 50 GB being the industry standard for feature-length film. They can store hours of video in High-Definition 1080P and Ultra High-Definition 2160P, also known as 4K UHD. Up to 60 frames per second. They have the highest quality audio and support 3D formatting as well. Even their packaging is smaller than DVD. Modern Blu-ray players are backward-compatible, in that they can play DVD's as well. All recent Sony PlayStation consoles can play them. It's a super-powerful format of film, offering the finest home video experience. At the end of the day, how does Blu-ray fair against VHS? Well, obviously they obliterate them quality-wise. It's the difference between a Formula 500 Racecar and a 2002 Honda Civic. No contest. But how about collectability? Sure, there are millions of Blu-ray collectors. The thing is, as a *collectible* they have their shortcomings: price, scarcity, and nostalgia. When it comes to price, special-release editions of bad B-movie classics can go from anywhere between $25 - $50. Because DVD's are still being produced, many opt for the DVD version at half that price. Also, they're not scarce at all; stores and malls still sell them.

Only those previously mentioned special releases can be harder to find at times, and even then, most can be discovered online. When it comes to nostalgia, they're too recent to hold any place in people's hearts. They were merely at the tail-end of the video store, which brings us to the last point: Many people began switching over to digital streaming right after Blu-ray came out. In a way, they suffer from the physical medium being made obsolete entirely. They are the last hurrah of home video, and thus must compete with the dying of physical film ownership; a heavy burden to bear.

HD DVD

Short for "High Definition Digital Versatile Disc", HD DVD was primarily developed and pushed by Toshiba in an attempt to upgrade and succeed over regular DVD. HD DVD-ROM had a single-layer capacity of 15 GB and a dual-layer capacity of 30 GB. They could support 720p, 1080i, and 1080p video. For audio, they could support up to 24-bit/192 kHz for two channels of audio, or up to eight channels of 24-bit/96 kHz encoding. Beginning as a competitor to Blu-ray in 2006, the "format war" between the two lasted roughly two years. They were quite similar as far as quality goes, and as you can imagine there are many analogies to the previous VHS/Betamax war of the 1980s. For about two solid years you could find video stores and shops selling both HD DVD and Blu-ray, as they were unsure of which would dominate. In the end, Blu-ray won. The main factor behind this wasn't mere consumer preference, but an alliance of various companies banding together to throw support behind one format. Once Sony (with its PlayStation 3 console) along with other film studios (such as Warner Bros, New Line Cinema, Walt Disney and 20th Century Fox) fully shifted into support for Blu-ray, the writing was on the wall. By 2008, Toshiba threw in the towel and HD DVD was no more. As far as collectability, there's little to no demand due to several reasons. There's not a ton of titles, nor is there much to romanticize. HD DVD lost the format war too quickly. They were only around for two short years, and most consumers who bet on HD DVD were left feeling like losers. Second-hand HD DVD players can still be purchased online, along with the films. Being such a recent loss, there's no real nostalgia for it. Due to having such a limited film catalog, you can firmly plant HD DVD in the realm of the video dead. Compared to VHS or DVD collecting, it's six feet under with nobody even visiting its grave.

DVD

Digital Versatile Disc (DVD) began development in 1995 and released publicly in 1996. As mentioned in the second chapter, it was a complete game-changer. While they could store any type of digital data, it was most prolific in the world of home video. They could hold up to 8.5 GB on a single-sided double-layer disc, and twice that for double-sided discs. In other words, they could easily fit one or two long-running films, behind-the-scenes featurettes, alternate audio tracks, and so on. The playback was smooth and practically flawless. The audio could range from mono to 5.1 surround sound, all depending on the film. It was not only superior to VHS, but to Laserdisc as well. For a full decade, it was just about the highest quality format you could own a movie on. They came in small packages, often with bonus artwork layered inside the case. Throughout the late 1990s to the early millennium, DVD reigned supreme. Even the technically superior Blu-ray wasn't a deathblow to DVD. In fact, it wasn't until nearly 2017 when streaming services surpassed DVD and Blu-ray sales. To this day they can be easily found by the hundreds in various retail chains across North America and are still in mass production. So how do they fare against VHS as far as collectability? Well, because so many 20-somethings grew up as kids renting them from Blockbuster, they certainly do have some semblance of retro-nostalgia. One great factor is the price point;

they're still found dirt cheap everywhere from garage sales to thrift stores. It's common to find rare B-movies for a couple of bucks. Ironically, this is the main factor preventing it from taking hold as a prime collectible: they're not scarce. Not at all. It's hard to collect something if there's very little "rare-factor" to it. You might describe it as still existing in a sort of fun and easy-going collectible stage. Yes, there are a few distribution companies whose film output is sought after, but most DVD releases are not unique or fawned over. Overall, DVD's are certainly collectible, albeit it tends to be in a more *casual* way, at least compared to VHS.

Laserdisc

The first home video optical disc format, Laserdisc (or "LD"), was created and sold by MCA DiscoVision beginning in 1978. It was developed surprisingly early, in the late 1960s/early 70s, yet never took the market by storm. They were 12-inch discs — so for the uninitiated, picture giant discs the size of vinyl records (only heavier!). They could store roughly 60 minutes of video per side, with a horizontal resolution of 425 TVL lines for NTSC. To put that in perspective, VHS had 240 TLV, so LD was certainly higher quality. They also used a variety of surround sound formats in PCM 16-bit and 44.056 kHz.

Essentially CD-quality audio. They were far superior to their VHS and Beta rivals. So, what happened? *Price-point* was the main concern for consumers. A good Laserdisc player could cost hundreds of dollars, sometimes closer to $1,000 USD. Adjust that for inflation and you can see the obvious problem. Compared to the price of a VCR, it was no contest. Hundreds of dollars for Laserdisc, or a fraction of that for the abundant and prolific VHS. Although LD did achieve success throughout Asia, it never really caught on throughout North America. The very last Laserdisc was manufactured in 2000. So, how does Laserdisc fair as far as collectability goes? Well, because they were around for quite some time, coupled with the nostalgia of many folks *remembering* them being in video stores (but never *owning* them), they are still fairly desired today. Most LD players can be found relatively cheap, and horror/b-movies on LD can fetch a pretty penny. One problem is that the discs themselves are rather fragile; if not taken care of, they can warp and skip just as bad as old music CDs. Their large cover art looks fantastic in a collection and some specific titles are getting harder to find. They had a limited-but-decent run throughout the US, and so the rare-factor for many films keep prices at a competitive rate. Although LD reaches nowhere near the desirability of VHS, Laserdiscs are certainly something to watch out for, especially key genre films and rarer Japanese versions.

Betamax

The early competitor to VHS, Betamax (or "Beta") was a magnetic videotape format originally developed by Sony in 1975. The tapes were smaller than VHS, measuring in at 6 1/7 × 3 3/4 × 1 inches. Although different versions could record different lengths, the average Betamax tape could hold roughly 5-hours of video. By 1985 their tapes could produce up to 290 lines on a regular-grade Beta cassette — slightly superior to VHS. They became a standard in TV broadcasting, but severely struggled in the home video market. They entered into a "format war" where both platforms fought tooth-and-nail for a place in consumers' homes. While it took years before VHS dominated the video store shelf entirely, it was inevitable that only one medium would survive. Through a string of marketing blunders and business mistakes, Beta eventually lost entirely. VCRs became more prevalent and home recording more commonplace. Once the dominoes began to fall, it was all but too late; VHS emerged a winner. By the late 1980s, it was rare to even find them in stores. Although blank Betamax tapes were technically manufactured up to 2016 and Sony Betamax players up to 2002, good luck finding consumers who used them past 1990. VHS conquered the market long ago.

Compared to VHS collectability, how does Betamax fare? Since many early (and now rare) films were released on Beta, there are *still* collectors hunting them down. While it is getting harder to find Beta tapes at all, that only adds fuel to the fire. It's not uncommon to find them in VHS collections; where VHS is found, there's often a chance of finding a few Beta tapes mixed in. On the other hand, *working* Beta players are becoming quite rare. Many have broken down over the decades and are surprisingly difficult to repair. A working Beta player can be worth hundreds if in good shape. Tapes can still be found on eBay and in collecting circles — albeit nowhere near as commonly as VHS. At the end of the day, it's safe to say that *yes*, some Betamax releases are quite desirable — but *no*, it simply doesn't come with the same fervor as VHS collecting. There's a passion for VHS that is still unrivaled. Beta lost the war and will never achieve VHS status, even postmortem.

CED/Videodisc

Capacitance Electronic Disc (or more widely known as CED or Videodisc) was a brief and often forgotten analog video disc format created by RCA. Despite being initially designed in 1964, due to technical and marketing problems CED didn't see commercial release until 1981. By that time, VHS and Beta were dominating the home video market. Although it physically resembled Laserdisc, they were technically closer to vinyl records in that they weren't read with a laser but with a needle-like stylus. They could hold 1-hour on each side, with about 27,000 still frames per side. Although RCA had high hopes for the format, Videodisc only lasted about four short years before the company called it quits in 1984. As you might guess, a ton of money was lost. In that time, they had manufactured over 1,500 different film titles and close to 750,000 players. The discs themselves looked cool in design, however, they were rife with playback problems - any dust on the inner disc or degradation of the stylus would cause frames to skip. Today, it's extremely hard to find a Videodisc player that doesn't have terrible playback.

So, how does CED fair against VHS collecting? It has both pros and cons. The *pros* would be their scarcity, unique design, and often cheap price point. Visually, they look like giant floppy discs with movie artwork plastered across them. Retro-futuristic and weird, indeed! They can often be found for $5–10 dollars each, depending on genre or title. With such a limited production run they do have a "rare-factor" to them. The *cons* would be its small film catalog, coupled with the fact that most CED players have downright awful playback. At least with HD DVD or Betamax, you're getting a collectible you can watch. Yes, they have great aesthetic and make excellent conversation pieces to display in a collection. However, they were an unknown and unwanted format for a reason: impractical and usually inoperable, they were possibly the biggest loser format of all time. They were simply dead on arrival.

There were other brief and limited CD-ROM-style formats and videodiscs; however, the above formats are the most centrally recognized mediums of home video. They're all collectible in some way or another, but VHS and DVD take the lead. To re-iterate something mentioned earlier, each step forward left something behind. In other words, not all films released on VHS went to DVD, not all films on DVD went to Blu-ray, and so on. VHS still has the most prolific film roster, along with a retro-factor. DVDs are still being produced. It's missing the rarity and uniqueness of VHS and because of that reason, tapes are still king of the collectibles. Keep in mind, it's not uncommon to find other formats within any film buff's collection. Always be on the lookout for alternative releases of various movies — be it top-of-the-line limited edition Blu-ray releases or dust-covered formats that have been lost to time. Especially if the price is right!

12. Vanishing Point

Whether we're talking about VHS, Betamax, or any tape-based format, magnetic tape itself will only last so long. There were only so many VHS manufactured as well. Is it possible for VHS to eventually vanish altogether? How about the sale of tapes within modern-day stores? What about mold? Should you really invest all your money into rare VHS instead of a proper retirement savings portfolio? FYI, your family is going to freak out if they find you asking the latter.

While it's not a fun thing for collectors to think about, there are experts who claim that magnetic tape has an expiration date. 1/4-inch reel-to-reel audiotape from the 1960s and 70s is already degrading. Many claim VHS has a shelf-life of an additional decade or so. The problem is that "they" have been saying this for a while. Back in the early 2000s, many folks predicted that by 2010-2015 most VHS would be disintegrated beyond watchability. At the time of this writing, old VHS tapes still play quite well. Multimedia transfer companies (businesses that transfer old film formats to digital) will unanimously tell you that VHS has a shelf life of about 10-25 years.

Others will tell you that they degrade at about 1 - 2% per year. So, a tape from 1990 should be about 30% more degraded today than on the day you purchased it. *Or so they say...*

It seems it's nearly impossible to put a serious number on it. Most predictions have been completely wrong. Not only that, but other factors play a more significant role in their degeneration. The number of times you play a tape affects its longevity. Ever notice a nude scene on tape flicker or dwindle in quality? That's because the person who last watched or rented it had paused and rewound that scene multiple times. The more you watch and replay a VHS, the less the magnetic tape holds up. Simple as that.

Aside from wear-and-tear due to playback, the most common issue facing tape preservation is mold. As previously mentioned, the magnetic tape used inside VHS is prone to white mold. This only occurs when tapes are stored in cool and damp areas. While it's totally preventable, it's also super common to find tapes stowed in garages, sheds, crawlspaces, attics, barns and outdoor storage units. Many people simply tossed their VHS and Beta into cardboard boxes and stashed them away in less-than-ideal locations. This has led to countless tapes developing the sinister spores. Although they can usually be cleaned, it's certainly not optimal. Once mold has breached beyond the surface level of magnetic tape, it's often unsalvageable. This can all be prevented by keeping your VHS tapes indoors and away from damp and humid areas. The drier the better.

There has been some confusion in regard to VHS Rewinders. As you might recall, those were small (sometimes battery-powered) rewinding machines that did one thing only: rewind tapes. For some reason, many folks assume this was to help preserve the tapes themselves. No, it was to help ease the wear-and-tear on VCRs. In fact, some rewinding machines spun so hard that they would cause the magnetic tape to rip-off at the end of the cycle. *Not good.* Buyer beware: you're better off using a cheap second VCR if you're that concerned about VCR preservation. Many VCRs can tell when it's near the end/start of the tape and will automatically slow down the rewinding process in order to not damage it.

Overall, it's not that hard to keep a VHS collection in decent shape. Keep them dry and rewind carefully with a good VCR. In fact, use a good VCR cleaner every now and then. The tape heads (mechanical devices inside the machine) need to be cleaned. Don't stack VHS on top of one another horizontally. So many people do this, and it is bad practice. Imagine the combined pressure of 50+ tapes all pressing down on the bottom few. Although the plastic is strong, it is possible for cases to crack and for plastic to warp. Display them standing up. It's a good habit to get into. Also, try to avoid direct sun exposure. That's why so many big boxes and cardboard slipcases have faded artwork - they were kept near a window, with direct (or even indirect) sunlight on them. Slowly over the years, the colorful artwork on many tapes has faded away. These small tips will help ensure your collection will last many more years to come.

Sure, that's all fine and dandy for those with a collection, but what about newbies who are having trouble *finding* tapes altogether? The last chapter of this book will give you some tips and tricks regarding tape hunting. However, many thrift stores and surviving mom-and-pop shops no longer stock VHS. Every day, eBay prices get higher as more and more stores liquidate whatever VHS stock they have left. Popular hunting grounds such as Goodwill thrift stores have unanimously decided to stop carrying tapes altogether. Most pawnshops have dumped almost all their VHS stock. Typically, those stores only receive common post-1997 releases and Disney clamshells — the kinds of tapes most collectors scoff at. Over time, their tapes have sat on the shelf too long for them to justify carrying VHS inventory altogether. It's unfortunate because it's only now that many people who are around the age where they can start collecting (i.e. out of college, live on their own, working full time, etc.) are also able to experience nostalgia for home video of the 80s and 90s.

The decade from 2000 – 2010 was a great time for tape hoarders. Thrift stores, pawnshops and flea markets were *gold mines* for old and obscure VHS. Hundreds of video rental stores had gone out of business and sold off huge stockpiles of tapes. Hindsight is 20/20 of course, and that's part of the reason tapes are worth what they're worth. The same goes for any collectible; how many times have you heard baby boomers say something like, "Oh, I had all those old 1950s Spiderman and Superman comic books, but your grandmother threw them all away!" If we only knew better. That sentiment is what both nags and spurs on the collecting mentality.

The future of VHS is a rough one, as it certainly has the odds stacked against it. Tapes are fallible and fragile (at least compared to DVD/Blu-ray). They're harder and harder to find by the day. However, that's what separates the wheat from the chaff; where most people are willing to give up their minuscule collections for a cheap price, others are willing to buy. It's the serious collectors who go the extra mile, dig deeper into that dust-covered bin, and get down on their hands and knees at that old antiques barn. If you want to amass a great VHS horde in the year 2020, you've got to be willing to get your hands dirty! Think of it as an escapade — half the fun is the exploratory process. Once again, the thrill of the hunt is just as important as the acquisition. Of course, there is another option: money and an internet connection. But where's the fun in that?

Despite 30-somethings being the most notable age bracket in tape collecting, the most impressive collections today are typically owned by those in their 40's. Just something to consider: not only do they have the most disposable income, but also the largest real estate. Throughout most North American cities, prices of detached houses have gone through the roof (no pun intended). Because of this, Millennials (those in their late-20's and 30's) tend to be relegated to apartments, condos and small townhouses. Their physical display space is often limited, as opposed to Gen-X'ers who not only tend to have more display space but have also had more time to accumulate tapes over the years. This isn't a rule by any means, just a general observation.

Speaking of age demographics, what happens when those folks who remember VHS and video stores simply dwindle in numbers? For example: there was a brief window of time when 8-Track (an old style of audiotape) was considered a collectible. That time has long since passed. 8-tracks were popular in the late 1960s/early 70s. Those who are old enough to remember music stores *selling* 8-track tapes are mostly senior citizens today. Many of those tapes have physically degraded beyond having any real value. The days of hunting down that antiquated audio format are over. Nobody lusts after 8-tracks anymore. Vinyl records are an exception, as they never ceased production. At some point, VHS collecting will hit a wall where there will be very few folks who remember or care about tapes. The digitally based youth of tomorrow ("iGen" or "Generation Y") won't have a clue what magnetic tape is. A decade from now and VHS will be so obscure and hard to find that Millennials who have yet to start collecting *simply never will*. Think about that. Desirable VHS films will be so rare and so expensive that collecting them en masse pretty much won't happen. Tapes are only going up in value. If you don't get in *now* while the price is still somewhat affordable, just wait until demand rises and many tapes become even *more* scarce. Most collectors will probably tell you that prices are too high *today*. What about tomorrow? What about a decade from now?

Much like Beanie Babies, it would be unwise to suggest VHS tapes are any sort of actual investment. Sure, an item is worth whatever someone is willing to pay. Yes, anything can be "a collectible". Just consider that anyone who was alive in the late 1990s will tell you what a silly thing Beanie Babies were: plush toys that made American investors lose their minds. People thought they were worth hundreds, even thousands of dollars apiece. For a very brief window of time, they *were*, but that bubble quickly burst and reality came crashing down. They were not useful in any way, shape or form. They were simply not real investments, period. At the end of the 90s, they suddenly became worthless overnight. You can argue that golden-age comic books are legitimate investments; however, you would have to have gotten in years ago to really make it worthwhile. Most rare comics haven't skyrocketed in price recently, although admittedly a few have (due to popular theatrical adaptations). Either way, should you choose to invest a thousand dollars into *Tales from The QuadeaD Zone* or *The Texas Chainsaw Massacre* on Astral clamshell — good luck! A decade from now, it might not be a sellers' market.

Even if VHS and all its collectors eventually disappear, are there any positives to the modern platform of digital streaming? So far, we've only mentioned the negative aspects of services like Netflix — the loss of video stores, the force-feeding of film recommendations, and the avoidance of exposure to terrible cinema. It's easy to live in a perfect digital film bubble, but of course, there are obvious upsides to it. Cheap and easy access to thousands of movies is something we only dreamt about in the 80s and 90s. The adventure of searching for and hunting down specific films may be a thing of the past, but the joy of *watching* them remains as strong as ever. Folks who previously had no exposure to certain movies (due to restrictions or even financial limitations) now have access to thousands of films. YouTube vloggers mock bad movies as we all did back in the day with our friends. Plus, there are hundreds of those online reviewers. The idea that you can now sort out the good-bad films from the unwatchable trash has saved many film fans from a ton of headaches. There are online fan-lists of bad movies, good movies, director recommendations, etc. along with solid suggestions based on films you already like. Of course, this can feed into the "bubble" aspect, omitting films you would have never watched had you only stuck to the recommended playlists. Then again, most people don't rigidly stick to algorithmic recommendations. Most folks still enjoy random selections, even given a near-infinite stream of choices.

Compiling tapes is perhaps the single reason remnants of video stores still exist within the zeitgeist of North America. Many collectors have cultivated collections so epic that they not only work as time capsules of the pre-2000s but as a historic cache of film culture itself. A well-assembled mock video store (or any significant retro collection for that matter) can be truly inspirational, providing instant nostalgia for anyone who steps foot in the room. It immediately takes you back to a time of face-to-face interactions, conversations and even arguments over movies and cinema. It can serve as an educational display for a younger generation — a generation that is often surprisingly enthusiastic and curious about movie rental stores. For many kids, it's a foreign concept but not one void of charm.

In some cases, complete distributor-specific collections have never even *existed* outside of the original manufacturing warehouse. Video stores carried a mixed catalog of distributors. To see a completed set of any specific catalog in a streamlined display is more than just rare. In some cases, a well-curated and uniquely targeted VHS collection may be the only one of its existence anywhere in the world. Many of these collectors have the only firm and solid record of who released what, and when.

There is a certain responsibility to archiving a specific time, product or format. Many of the best museums that deal with hyper-specific collections are privately owned. You might imagine that there's some open-to-the-public institution that is just full of original VHS releases. Nope. Although there are small VHS and film exhibits, video store recreations that have extensive tape collections are almost always privately owned.

It may sound melodramatic, but VHS collectors truly are the curators of a lost aspect of our art and culture. While there are valid arguments against the broader idea of retro-nostalgia (i.e. rigidly holding onto the past for personal affections vs. forward-thinking progression of a genre or culture), most folks collect for healthy reasons. It's an effort to procure art and entertainment of a previous era. It's a celebratory action. Most tape collectors are not literally "hoarders" in the psychological or medical sense. They're hoarding and amassing tapes in order to preserve the forgotten 1980s and 1990s film community. People love a good "blast from the past," and that golden age of home video lives on within the basements and studios of collectors around the world.

For those who are just pondering the idea: is it a good idea to *start* collecting tapes in 2020?

Absolutely! Whether you're a casual film fan wanting to build up a small and specific collection, or just someone with an affinity for the video stores of yesteryear, now is the time to start. Not next year. Not next summer. *Now*. Like many things in life, *time* is the secret sauce. Patience is key. Get started early and enjoy the search. If you make it a hobby and not a goal, you'll be all the happier.

     Yes, eventually VHS will disappear from thrift stores entirely. Even pawnshops will have tossed out all those Disney clamshells. Grandpa's stockpile of home videos will have rotted away behind the radiator, forming a smoldering and grotesque pile of plastic grime. Hordes of *Titanic* and *Jerry Maguire* tapes will be found floating in a garbage patch in the middle of the Atlantic Ocean. Rest assured, there are folks who have kept their tapes in pristine condition. Those tapes are dusted and cleaned regularly, cataloged and placed perfectly on proper shelving. Warm and dry, they're displayed in all their glory. Those folks are the proverbial mutant tape hoarders — cultivators of a lost community. They work to preserve not only stories on tape, but the story of our society and its lost love of home video.

13. Attack of The Tapeheads

If the core of what defines a culture and community are the people involved in maintaining it, then we really should hear from a few members within the VHS community. These folks are the mortar upon which the house is built, the foundation of a VHS nation. Salt of the earth, tape hoarders at their best! This will be a mix of North American collectors from different age groups. They've been asked to say a few words on why the hobby and format have value and what the community means to them. Hopefully, it provides personal insight into the hearts of minds of those folks who find not only enjoyment but deeper meaning to the lost world of home video:

Dan Kinem (28)

"The video store meant so much to me as a kid. It was an event and I would always get so excited to go. It felt like an endless assortment of movies and I wanted to watch everything. It was also family bonding. We would all pick out a movie each and bring them back and watch all night. It's when I saw my first favorite movies and why I love movies in

general. My favorite night was watching Basket Case *and* Fargo *for the first time with my dad. Where I grew up there were two video stores a block away from me, literally in the same parking lot. I would go there all the time and look through the covers. It is still a memory I remember so well.*

My current collection is over 3000 tapes and is mostly focused on extremely rare and obscure shot on video and homemade movies. I love the idea that someone gathered up everyone they knew, made an entire movie, and went through the effort to release it on VHS with artwork. That's my favorite stuff. But I also love obscure releases and interesting companies. I have some favorite companies that I try to find everything they released because generally, it's all cool stuff. I never stop looking for movies and learning more each day which is why VHS is the best. They mean so much. It's my favorite thing in the world still after a decade of hardcore collecting. I've met so many people because of VHS, been all over North America because of VHS, still make a living because of VHS, etc. I still travel the country looking for them and I still buy new stuff all the time. I just got home with about 4000 tapes, mostly to sell, but some insanely cool stuff to keep. It's getting harder to find stuff I need but there's still thousands of things I want, and the hunt never stops."

Maurice Kenny (53)

"In 1979, the video store was the future, period. Something amazing was about to happen to the consumers who loved their idiot-box. Even in 1980, we grade-schoolers would excitedly talk about the fall movie premiers on TV during the viewer rating weeks. Only a few lucky friends owned a VCR and had a membership to rent tapes. They were not rich families but that's where they spent their money. They welcomed all kinds of kids into their house to watch Conan the Barbarian *and* Alien. *Movies on TV were now a waste of time as they were likely edited for content and full of commercials ("washroom breaks" as we called them). I convinced my father to rent a Beta machine and we figured out how to set it up and play the thing. Hard to believe, but renting a machine was the norm before video fever took hold and everyone had to own one. There was even one video store in downtown Brampton that only rented RCA Video Discs (or CED). My father made a Beta VCR purchase in 1983 while I continued to rent VHS to watch at my friend's house. B&J Video on McMurchy Ave. in Brampton, Ontario was where we got our membership, as they had a ton of Beta and VHS. For years that store was B-movie central. They had obscure American tapes that no other local stores dared to stock like* Make Them Die Slowly.

It was funny how one guy would rent the fantasy movies, while another grabbed the teen sex comedies. I focused on horror. The video store was our library, where we read the back covers and studied the artwork while trying to make an informed decision. As renting got cheaper, we became more impulsive and dared each other to rent anything. We often tricked others into renting movies like Fiend *or* Frankenstein Island, *then laughed our heads off as they cursed our recommendations. We started to notice we could trust renting Embassy Home Entertainment, Vestron, Media and my favorite, Thorn EMI.* Dawn of the Dead, Scanners, The Thing *and* Evil Dead *were thrilling experiences and it was very common for us to watch movies multiple times with different people. While TV and theater still played a role in our lives, the video store gave us access to everything. It really saved all those movies from being junked and forgotten about once its drive-in or regional theatrical run was over. Our local store provided free movie posters, promotional items and kept its attraction right up to when the big chains had displaced most others. In Brampton, Jumbo Video was huge. Circus Circus was fun. Video 99 was everywhere, and Ambassador Video had the largest horror section.*

When Blockbuster and Rogers Video muscled their way in, you were more likely to get a copy as they had so many doubles. The independents had to drop their prices substantially to compete. As DVD took hold, the magic of the video store was over, but my personal collection was now taking off via garage sales and clearance events. I regret not trying harder to get old VHS tapes of movies I had already seen, as I had made VHS and Beta copies and was now interested in the re-mastered Anchor Bay and uncut DVD versions. Tapes were being purged from homes as they were just another unwanted dust collector. Internet downloads, video-on-demand and movie streaming sites slowly eliminated the video store altogether.

From 2014 to 2019 my collection of dead media has quadrupled. My desire to have a video store of my own has been realized in a nostalgic way. I now have four basement rooms packed with alphabetized movie titles from every genre, organized with authentic video store racking. The walls are covered in CED's, posters and recordable videotape artwork. I am fully stocked with multiple format machines and movie collectibles like my Vestron Video promotional Re-Animator *paperweight. I enjoy showing off my Mom & Pop video store, so to speak. I literally have thousands of unwatched movies to select from, which I like to call 'Moeflix' as I have no satellite, cable or internet in the house. I have, however, joined the Facebook VHS collecting culture through my phone; I can be reached at Mauricecan66 at gmail dot com."*

Dario Smagata-Bryan (20)

"Local video stores were a big part of my childhood. Jumbo Video and Blockbuster were our local ones and the corner stores all rented films then, too. It was a routine every Friday to go to the video store and pick out something to watch that night. This was in the early 2000s though, and they had already stopped renting VHS tapes by then. So, all the movies I rented as a kid were on DVD, but all the movies I owned were on VHS, and those were the ones I cared more about! We couldn't afford to buy any new DVDs, so I grew up with VHS as my main source – renting DVDs was like a privilege. I'd search the thrift stores and pick up tapes for a quarter, and by doing that I built up an unusual taste in movies that has stuck with me ever since.

My current VHS collection has a wide range of genres, eras, and even languages. The only common thread is that they're all obscure movies, low budget releases and other stuff that went under the radar. I don't collect Hollywood blockbusters. Growing up I was always attracted to those weird titles on the video store shelves and I liked not knowing what to expect when going into a movie. As a VHS collector, I've stuck to that same idea and I've found a lot of hidden gems. That said, I'm not overly concerned with collecting well-known rare or valuable tapes – often the most expensive rarities are terrible movies! I do own some of the more famous and expensive VHS titles, but there are others in my collection that mean a lot more to me. There's no single factor that determines whether I want a certain title or not, it all depends, and I've never been able to make a 'want-list' for that reason. Currently, my main goals are to get the complete sets of Emmeritus Productions and Interglobal Video releases, but I'm always looking for other things and there are many that I won't even know I want until I see them.

As 2020 approaches, it's nice to see that VHS isn't such a dead format anymore. When I was growing up, DVD was reaching its peak and VHS tapes were being disposed of all over the place. That's why I was able to start collecting them, but it also meant there was very little interest, and it seemed like I was the only one after them. Now, of course, there's much more competition to find sought-after titles, but there's also a great community of other collectors to trade and talk tapes with. Because it's a relatively new hobby, the foundational knowledge is still being built, but there's so much more information available now than there was even a few years ago. The ability to discuss and learn from other collectors is huge in any hobby and it's really helped the VHS community to grow. I hope it'll keep on growing and that the core community of collectors will stay intact as time goes on."

Will Foran (27)

"I actually had a few local video stores that I frequented based on where I was in the city at the time. Each one brought with it a different atmosphere and excitement because no two stores were the same. There was the much-maligned Blockbuster Video, which typically meant I was after a new release, or my favorite Bonanza Video – which came after a dentist appointment visit and had the best stock of retro video games to go along with its film selection. My best friend growing up also had a store out near his house that his parents' friends owned, and it had a massive horror section we would walk through. A lot of the covers caught my eye then. Really, what these stores meant to me growing up was a way to escape the

mediocrity of middle school and dive into a nerdy movie night with my best friend where copious amounts of junk would be consumed. The fact that I can still recall the Alien, Terminator 2, Wayne's World *triple feature I think is an indication that renting movies had a profound effect on me.*

My current VHS collection is probably hovering around 900-1000 tapes. I haven't counted in a while. I'd like to try and keep it at that number because I'm starting to run out of space, but the trouble is that I'm so attached to these magnetic slabs that I'll surely need to find more room sooner than later. The short version of how I've gotten to where I'm at now would be that I started off grabbing VHS as a cheap way to enjoy some of my favorite films. As I started to uncover rare or out of print oddities, it became a full-fledged hobby – with Canadian films and distributors being the centerpiece of it all. With VHS collecting blowing up as it has, it also turned me on to a lot of shot on video and underground films that I might have never discovered. Some of the tapes I've acquired that fall into that latter category have become some of my favorites. Seeing as it's almost 2020, some may want to continue to write off VHS as dead and gone. While the nostalgia is part of the fun, I more so like to think of my hobby as a way to discover the underappreciated gems that I never got a chance to see, being too young to really enjoy the VHS heyday through the 1980s. Some of my favorite films came into view for the first time for me on VHS and I think without the underground fanatics really shilling for these old movies we wouldn't be seeing all the Blu-ray rereleases coming out now. There is a place for VHS in the future and I'll be happy to be a part of wherever this weird hobby is headed as we continue to move further and further away from analog."

These are just a few of the hundreds (or perhaps thousands) of serious VHS collectors across North America. Most folks simply fly under the radar, accumulating and amassing collections that are only known amongst their friends and family. Not everyone puts themselves "out there"; however, everyone contributes to the community in different ways. For example, there are documentaries such as *Adjust Your Tracking* and *Rewind This* which showcase a variety of collectors, their history, and the broader philosophy of VHS collecting. Podcasts such as "The VHS Bandits" not only review films on tape but also discuss the artwork and tape swaps, and interview fellow collectors. Parody YouTubers such as "The Cinema Snob" and his Big Box segments review classic big box artwork along with the movie. Websites such as www.VHScollector.com make a serious attempt to document and categorize VHS distribution companies and their releases. Blogs such as www.critcononline.com discuss VHS distribution companies in-depth, alongside traditional film and genre critiques. *VHS Hoarders* is an online show documenting the personal collections of hardcore collectors. There are fans across North America hosting community tape-swaps, VHS meetups, and viewing parties. This book itself is a small attempt to contribute to the community and help perpetuate the forgotten platform. When we take a step back and view all this at a distance, it's obviously so much more than just "collecting tapes in a room". It's an entire *society* of fans, friends, and family, transcending beyond age and country. A memorialization of our civilizations lost form of entertainment: VHS tape!

14. Be Kind — Rewind

So, you want to be a mutant tape hoarder, eh? Of course not! However, if you've made it this far into the book, you're either thinking about casually collecting VHS, already a serious collector or simply have a bizarre thirst for knowledge. Either way, this final chapter is here to help you in any tape hunting endeavors. The golden age of finding rare VHS for dirt cheap prices might be gone, but there are still many ways to amass an excellent collection without breaking the bank. Plenty of tips and tricks — especially for those able to think outside the box and willing to get their hands dirty! Okay, let's plunge right into it.

Family & Friends: The most basic and obvious way to find tapes. Thing is, it's easy to miss what is hidden in plain sight. Many folks simply forget that their loved ones often have small and unwanted collections tucked away in their basements. Sure, it's mostly junk; however, often there's at least *one* decent tape hidden in that dusty old box. One vintage horror or B-movie that everyone in the house forgot about. It's just sitting there, in the dark. Because they're your friends and family, they're usually more than happy to just give it to you. Worst case scenario, you owe them a thank you card. They probably don't even have a VCR in the house to watch them on. If they do, offer to take *that* off their hands as well. Save them a trip to the dump, right? Talk within your social circle and mention how you're collecting VHS. You'd be surprised how often close acquaintances offer you their old tapes without even being asked. After all, what are friends for?

Garage Sales: Most residents in your neighborhood and surrounding city have no clue *which* films are worth *what* exactly. To be fair, most don't even care. Take advantage of that. One man's trash is another's treasure! You'd be surprised how many collectors find absolute gems while hitting up local garage sales. Don't be afraid to ask outright if they have old VHS inside the house. 9 times out of 10 they'll say "no". However, that one single "yes" may be the biggest score of your life. You simply never know *who* has *what* stashed away in their basement. Swallow your pride and ask. When it comes to garage sales, sellers are usually looking to get rid of everything they can. Old VHS is often on the chopping block. Show up and take those unwanted tapes off their hands. Make them a deal! Also, don't forget dear, departed Grandma's old Betamax collection. *She* certainly won't be needing that anymore.

Flea Markets: As you might guess, most flea markets have been picked clean of rare tapes. Collectors have hit them hard over the last decade. That being said, there are constantly new booths every weekend. Sometimes they can have decent tapes; you never know. It's not as likely but when it happens, it happens. Also, note that it's *here* you can get the best bargains and prices. If you're looking for more common drama, action or comedy films and are willing to haggle, check the local flea market before anywhere else. You can probably build up a solid non-horror section for your collection at less than a dollar a pop. Buy in bulk if you can. Fifty cents per tape is often what collectors will bargain down to for "commons". Not a hard rule, just something to consider.

Antique Shops: Similar to flea markets, most of these places are void of tapes entirely. So why mention it? Well, when you do find some old antiques barn with VHS, it can be a goldmine. Because their focus is on everything being *antique*, they tend to avoid carrying post-millennium multimedia. So, when they do have tapes, they're usually quite old and therefore often on the rarer side. These shops usually don't check eBay sold listings for VHS, either. They embrace the thrill-of-the-hunt and celebrate the collecting community. This is a healthy motto, so never pass up the opportunity to rummage through those filthy old cardboard boxes. There are stories of tape hunters finding hundreds of rare big boxes in the back of some barn for *pennies* on the dollar. This is the part where you may have to get your hands dirty. Pro tip: bring cash and a flashlight!

<u>Thrift Stores</u>: Probably the most consistent source for cheap and more-common tapes in 2020. Even though franchises such as Goodwill have mostly stopped carrying VHS, most other thrift stores still do. The majority don't check eBay sold listings for specific films (probably only due to time constraints), and therefore you can still find desirable tapes for a buck or two. It's certainly not what it used to be; most rare gems have been scooped up and cherry-picked over the years. It's important to understand that *most* of these stores bring in and cycle through new donations, depending on sales. For example, if a store is selling a lot of VHS, they are incentivized to stock more of them in their inventory. They'll import used tapes from other stores, rotating through different titles and stock, while shipping out their old titles. This provides customers with a seemingly new set of inventory, and that is where you can take advantage. If you consistently hit all the thrift stores in your city on a regular basis (say, once every week or two), you can usually gather up a solid collection over a few years'

time. Patience is a virtue. Many collectors make the mistake of assuming they only re-stock shelves every other month or year. In reality, most strategically cycle through new inventory daily. If you notice that their VHS shelf has been neglected, you can always bite the bullet and try the following: Drop $20 or $30 on those unwanted tapes, donate them somewhere else, then visit back a few days later. Assuming they still choose to carry VHS, you'll find a brand-new shelf of tapes to mull over. It's a total gamble, but for some, it has paid off. If you want these stores to continue *selling* VHS, you need to demonstrate that there are customers still *buying* them.

    Pawn Shops: For many people, a pawn shop is the first place they think of when it comes to tape-hunting. The problem is you are not the first person to think of this. Most have been picked dry 10x over. Of course, every pawn shop is different, so don't ignore them entirely. Just don't expect to find much in the way of desirable titles. Most pawnshops have switched over to DVD and Blu-ray exclusively. Also, consider that most of these shops don't *buy* tapes, and therefore don't *sell* tapes. If they do, chances are they proactively check eBay/online sales and price accordingly. Feel free to occasionally peruse and patron these kinds of second-hand shops, just don't expect much. This chapter is here to help you save time as well as money.

Estate Sales: Essentially, these are large-scale garage sales, focusing on selling furniture and huge lots of homewares. Sometimes (though rarely) you can find large collections of multimedia being sold during these events. Not common, but there are stories of giant retro film and tape collections being auctioned off at blowout prices. Just something to consider. As you can imagine, this is not the way most folks build their VHS collection. Just know that tales of VHS acquisition via estate sales exist for a reason: they occasionally do happen! While you may not want to waste too much time chasing down these events (and you could very well toss storage auctions in here as well), you can always count on tapes to pop up in the most unexpected places. In fact, a good rule to follow is that the places other collectors skip are the places you should double-check.

Present-Day Video Stores: Yes, there are still some video stores in existence! Do an internet search for video stores in your city (assuming you're not in a rural community) and you'd be surprised what's out there. Sure, they'll mostly be selling DVDs, Blu-ray, T-shirts and film paraphernalia, but many have small VHS sections for local collectors. Sometimes even a large selection, depending on the market. Be sure to support these shops — they're helping to perpetuate physical film ownership and will be more than happy to help with your tape hunting. Ask about tape-swaps in town. Ask about other collectors in the area. Ask if you can put up a flyer on the wall. These stores love people in the community coming together (especially on their shop floor) and doing these kinds of things. Speaking of which...

Tape Swaps: By far the best way to find desirable titles at decent prices. Although these events don't often happen, when they *do* occur, they have great selection and value! It's pretty self-explanatory: these are organized VHS swaps and sales, usually taking place in the back of stores, theaters or public venues. They're a gathering of tapeheads with doubles and extras, ready to trade or make a deal. Depending on the turnout, it's usually VHS galore. Often the pinnacle event in tape collecting, these are nothing but fellow collectors sharing stories and selling the good stuff. Check online for events in a city near you. These are often referred to as "VHSwaps" or "VHStivals". Can't find any events in your city? *Start your own!* Find a local store (even a privately-owned coffee shop can suffice) open to the idea or rent out a cheap venue. Advertise on social media. Put up posters and flyers. Tell non-collectors that they can sell their old tapes for cash. Tell serious collectors you'll provide them with tables and vendor space. Make it as professional as possible and you'll often be surprised at the turnout. There could be dozens of collectors in your city who mistakenly assume that *because* there are no VHS events are taking place, there must be no other VHS collectors. Be the one to break that spell.

Social Media: The present-day hangout for collectors. If you're looking for rare stuff at a fair price, look no further than the following Facebook groups: "Horror VHS Collectors Unite!", "Planet VHS Horror!", and "VHS Collectors Canada". They have thousands of members with dozens of daily sales. There are tons of interesting topics, photos, and conversations. All it takes is an internet connection and social media account. Collectors typically want to help each other out and these are fantastic places to get started. Fire sales (fast-paced sales where hundreds of tapes are sold off quickly) are a frequent selling technique that can yield a patient collector *dozens* of films at low prices. Also, be sure to check out Instagram; although it has far fewer sales, you'll find the odd gem through it. It's also a great place to find out what's hot, discover who's who, and find interesting stories that might not hit Facebook. Even if you don't plan to buy or sell, it's just as useful for communicating with fellow collectors about anything and everything VHS related. Many of the photos posted throughout these sites are downright jaw-dropping — hundreds of ultra-rare collections and amazing displays. If anything, don't let jealousy get to you!

eBay: Typically, this is a collectors last resort. Although hundreds of common *and* rare tapes pass through this popular auction website daily, it's by far the most expensive. Expect high-ball prices with few actual deals. Shipping is a pain if you're in Canada or anywhere outside the United States. However, if you have the money and a PayPal account, you can usually find whatever your heart desires. Nothing wrong with using it, just keep in mind this is the place where prices are jacked up (which in turn spurs on higher pricing altogether). Many people live out in the middle of nowhere and have no other option. Perhaps others find their hometown simply has little-to-no tapes at all. It happens. For some, auction websites like eBay are their only choice. It's easy, but it isn't cheap! Amazon.com is another seller; however, in recent years their tape prices have been driven to crazy levels — assuming you can find decent tapes there at all.

There are no rules for collecting VHS. It's still the wild west in many respects, and thus a bit of ingenuity is recommended when hunting obscure titles. Know *when* and *where* to spend money on cheap commons. Have a plan (and the cash!) for when the rarer or more expensive titles pop up. The more fishing lines in the water, the more bites you'll get. Be proactive. Place "Wanted" ads on Craigslist and other classifieds. Save text-alerts for eBay searches. Put the word out to friends and family. Make it a fun ritual to hit the thrift stores every Sunday afternoon. The real way that huge collections are built is by strategic and relentless hunting.

Once you have a small collection, start on a case or display of some sort. How you display your collection, regardless of the items collected, makes all the difference! It's the distinction between *hoarding* tapes vs. *collecting* VHS. It will look so much better to your friends and family. It'll impress folks when they see photos of it. It can make it appear 100x more professional. Get some good shelving or racking, then go to town filling it up with all your old favorites. In fact, it's often a good idea to *start* with the display or racking! Speaking of which...

Final Tip: Don't pass on any retro video store-related paraphernalia, especially if you intend to seriously collect VHS. Things like big box protectors, posters, and cardboard standees are items that'll make your collection pop. Former store racks or standing isle-shelving are becoming *very* hard to find. When video stores disappeared, much of their display fixtures went with them. If you can find old signage, props, racks or displays, grab them! Another decade or so and they will be impossible to find. Don't have space? Do the right thing: alert fellow collectors when you discover them. There's a vibrant community out there who will not only purchase it but *display* it for the world to see!

As we've noted, it's the people who forge a community. Yes, tapes matter. The history of our culture matters. It all matters. However, if you're not engaged with the broader community — well, then you're just hoarding tapes in a basement. So, get out there! Hit up that local tape swap. Find a still-operating video store in your nearest city and spend a few moments talking to the owner. Join social media pages and start a conversation. Watch a VHS documentary with your significant other. Invite some friends over for some drinks and home-made pizza. Get them to pick out a great (or awful) tape from your collection, then have a blast regaling them with the instant nostalgia VHS provides. Many folks have forgotten the enjoyment of renting tapes and perusing through the local video store on a Saturday night.

Remind them.

Cory Gorski was born and raised in Ontario, Canada where currently lives with his wife and pet dog. An avid tape collector and film enthusiast, he can often be found on various related social media sites.